SOMALIA

UNENDING TURMOIL, SINCE 1975

AL J. VENTER

Pen & Sword

First published in Great Britain in 2017 by
PEN AND SWORD MILITARY
an imprint of
Pen and Sword Books Ltd
47 Church Street
Barnsley
South Yorkshire S70 2AS

Copyright © Al J. Venter, 2017

ISBN 978 1 52670 794 9

Typeset by Aura Technology and Software Services, India
Printed and bound in Malta by Gutenberg

Pen & Sword Books Ltd incorporates the imprints of Pen & Sword
Archaeology, Atlas, Aviation, Battleground, Discovery, Family History, History, Maritime, Military,
Naval, Politics, Railways, Select, Social History, Transport, True Crime, Claymore Press, Frontline Books,
Leo Cooper, Praetorian Press, Remember When, Seaforth Publishing and Wharncliffe.

For a complete list of Pen and Sword titles please contact
Pen and Sword Books Limited
47 Church Street, Barnsley, South Yorkshire, S70 2AS, England
email: enquiries@pen-and-sword.co.uk
website: www.pen-and-sword.co.uk

CONTENTS

Somali National Army soldier at Kismayo Military HQ. (Photo Tobin Jones)

TIMELINE

From a strategic trading zone on ancient Arab trading routes, through the turbulence of colonialism and Cold War rivalries and post-colonial political collapse, Somalia has had an eventful, if troubled, history. This is a chronology of key events in Somali history.

1500–1600
Portuguese traders land on the east coast of Africa and start intermittent power struggles with the Sultanate of Zanzibar for control of port cities and surrounding towns.

1840
The British East India Company signs treaties with the Sultan of Tajura for unrestricted trading rights.

1887
Britain reaches a final agreement with the local King Menelik II and various tribal chiefs, and draws a boundary with neighbouring Ethiopia to form British Somaliland. Besides trading interests, the British protectorate serves as a counterweight to the growing Italian influence in the key port city of neighbouring Zanzibar.

1897–1907
Italy makes several agreements with tribal chiefs and the British to finally mark out the boundaries of a separate Italian protectorate of Somaliland.

1908
Italy assumes direct administration of Italian Somaliland, giving the territory colonial status.

1936
Following decades of expansionism, Italy captures Addis Ababa and Ethiopia, which are merged with Italian Somaliland and Italian Eritrea to form the colony of Italian East Africa.

1940

June: Italian troops drive out the British garrison and capture British Somaliland.

1941

British and South African forces recapture British Somaliland and most of Italian Somaliland.

1947

Following Italy's defeat in the Second World War, Italy renounces all rights and titles to Italian Somaliland.

1950

The United Nations General Assembly adopts a resolution making Italian Somaliland a UN trust territory under Italian administrative control.

1941–1959

British Somaliland sees a period of colonial development as the territory moves towards a gradual development of local institutions and self-government.

1960

British and Italian Somaliland gain independence and merge to form the United Republic of Somalia.

1960–1969

Two successive democratically elected governments attempt to balance the expansionist interests of pro-Arab, pan-Somali factions with interests in Somali-inhabited areas of Ethiopia and Kenya, and with 'modernist' factions whose priorities include economic and social development.

1969

October: Major General Mohamed Siad Barre seizes power in a coup. Democratically elected President Abdirashid Ali Shermarke is assassinated.

1970

Barre declares Somalia a socialist nation and undertakes literacy programmes and planned economic development under the principles of 'scientific socialism'.

1972–1977

A period of persistent border clashes with Ethiopia for control of Ethiopia's Ogaden region. Severe drought in the region leads to widespread starvation.

1974

Somalia and the Soviet Union sign a treaty of friendship. Somalia joins the Arab League.

1977

Somalia invades the Ogaden region of Ethiopia.

1978

Following a gradual shifting of Soviet favour from Somalia to Ethiopia, and the infusions of Soviet arms and Cuban troops into Ethiopia, Somali troops are pushed out of Ethiopian territory.

1978–1990

A period of growing cooperation and strategic alliance between Somalia and the West begins. The United States becomes Somalia's chief partner in defence, training several Somali military officers in US military schools.

1991

At the end of a period of growing domestic factionalism, insurgency and an open war with clans in northwest Somalia, which have left the country in economic shambles and forced thousands of Somalis to flee their homes, Barre is ousted by opposition clans and forced to flee to Nigeria, where he ultimately dies.

1992

December: US troops lead a UN peacekeeping mission to Somalia under Operation Restore Hope, beginning with the arrival of 1,800 US Marines landing at night on a Mogadishu beach. The peacekeeping mission includes the provision of humanitarian assistance to Somalis and bringing peace to the troubled country. While the humanitarian mission is quickly achieved, however, the peacekeeping force finds itself dragged into Somalia's internecine battles.

1993

October: For the United States, Operation Restore Hope reaches its nadir when members of the US Army's elite Delta Force and the Army Rangers are used to raid warlord headquarters to abduct them. In one such raid, the US forces are dropped into a Mogadishu neighbourhood to snatch two lieutenants of warlord Mohamed Farrah Aidid. Whilst the snatch-and-grab operation is successfully accomplished, trouble starts when two US Sikorsky UH-60 Black Hawk helicopters are shot down by rocket-propelled grenades. As US Army Rangers attempt to rescue the crews of the downed helicopters, a mob of armed militiamen and angry Somalis descends on the site. Horrific carnage follows that ends only fifteen hours later when a combined US/UN armoured convoy manages to reach the trapped Rangers and Delta operators. But for the world, the mission in Somalia would forever be gruesomely remembered for the eighteen US Army Rangers killed and the footage of exultant crowds dragging their naked, mutilated bodies through the streets of Mogadishu. Despite domestic outrage, the US continues to play a major role in the mission until 1994.

1994

American President Bill Clinton orders the withdrawal of the 30,000 US troops stationed in Somalia.

1995

Following the withdrawal of US forces, the vanguard of the twenty-one-nation Operation Restore Hope, the UN peacekeepers, leaves after an unsuccessful operation, amidst charges of cruelty and even the murder of Somalis. By the end of the operation, dozens of UN peacekeepers are killed and hundreds of Somalis die at the hands of US and UN forces.

1997

Following a complete administrative collapse, chiefs of some rival clans meet in the Egyptian capital of Cairo where they agree to convene a conference to look into rival claims to Somalia.

2000

August: In the thirteenth such attempt to form a government, Somali warlords and militiamen meet in neighbouring Djibouti for peace talks organized by Djibouti President Omar Guelleh. They elect Abdulkassim

Salat Hassan president of Somalia. Hassan appoints Ali Khalif Galaydh as his prime minister. As the new government attempts to start the parliamentary process in exile in Djibouti, some powerful warlords, notably Hussein Mohammed Aideed and Mohamed Ibrahim Egal, do not recognize Hassan's election. Mogadishu's most powerful clan leader, Ali Mahdi Mohamed, however, promises his support.

October: Hassan arrives in Mogadishu to a hero's welcome and tight security. Galaydh puts together a cabinet of ministers, Somalia's first government in ten years. Hassan's administration, however, has difficulty establishing control outside Mogadishu.

2001

March: Aideed announces that he has patched up his differences with clan leaders Muse Sudi Yalahow and Osman Hassan Ali Atto and calls for a replacement of Hassan's transitional government following a meeting between the leaders in the Kenyan capital of Nairobi. Opposition to Hassan sees fighting rage in the southern parts of the country as drought, security concerns and the criminalization of refugee camps along the Somali–Kenyan border periodically compel Kenya to halt cross-border trade, thereby further crippling the economically crumbling East African country.

April: Somali warlords, backed by Ethiopia, decline to support transitional administration.

2004

August: In the fourteenth attempt since 1991 to restore central government, a new transitional parliament is inaugurated at a ceremony in Kenya. In October, the body elects Abdullahi Yusuf as president.

December: A tsunami off Indonesia displaces thousands on Somali coast.

2005

February–June: The Somali government begins returning home from exile in Kenya, but there are bitter divisions over where in Somalia the new parliament should sit. In November, Prime Minister Ali Mohammed Ghedi survives an assassination attempt in Mogadishu.

2006

February–May: The transitional parliament meets in the central town of Baidoa for the first time since it was formed in 2004. Shortly after, scores of people are killed and hundreds injured during fierce fighting between rival militias in Mogadishu, the worst violence in almost a decade.

June–July: Militias loyal to the Union of Islamic Courts take Mogadishu and other parts of the south after defeating clan warlords. Ethiopian troops enter Somalia.

July–August: Mogadishu's airports and ports are re-opened for the first time since 1995.

September: The transitional government and Islamic courts begin peace talks in Khartoum. Somalia's first known suicide bombing targets President Yusuf outside parliament in Baidoa.

December: Ethiopian and transitional government forces put Islamists to flight, capturing Mogadishu. A month later, Islamists abandon their last stronghold, the southern port of Kismayo. President Abdullahi Yusuf enters Mogadishu for the first time since taking office in 2004. This is followed by air strikes in the south against al-Qaeda figures, the first direct US military intervention in Somalia since 1993.

2007

March: After the UN Security Council authorizes a six-month peacekeeping mission, African Union troops land in Mogadishu amid pitched battles between Islamist insurgents and government forces backed by Ethiopian troops.

2008

May: The UN Security Council allows countries to send warships into Somalia's territorial waters to tackle pirates.

2009

January: Ethiopia completes its withdrawal of troops announced the previous year. Al-Shabaab capture Baidoa, formerly a key government stronghold. Meeting in Djibouti, parliament elects moderate Islamist Sheikh Sharif Sheikh Ahmed president, extending the transitional government's mandate for another two years.

May: Islamist insurgents launch an onslaught on Mogadishu and advance in the south. Al-Shabaab recaptures the southern port of Kismayo after defeating the rival Hizbul Islam militia.

2010–2012
Famine kills about a quarter of a million people, the UN says.

2010
February: Al-Shabaab formally declares an alliance with al-Qaeda, and begins to concentrate troops for a major offensive to capture the capital.

2011
January: In 2010, pirate attacks on ships worldwide hit a seven-year high, with Somali pirates accounting for forty-nine of the fifty-two ships seized. In July, the UN formally declares famine in three regions of Somalia. Al-Shabaab partially lifts a ban on foreign aid agencies in the south. The UN airlifts its first aid consignment to Mogadishu in five years. Al-Shabaab pulls out of Mogadishu in what it calls a 'tactical move'.

October: Kenyan troops enter Somalia to attack rebels they accuse of being behind several kidnappings of foreigners in Kenya. The American military begins flying drone aircraft from a base in Ethiopia. Ethiopian troops return to the central town of Guriel.

2012
February–May: Al-Shabaab loses the key towns of Baidoa and Afgoye to Kenyan, African Union and Somali government forces. In August, Somalia's first formal parliament in more than twenty years is sworn in at Mogadishu airport, ending the eight-year transitional period. Pro-government forces capture the port of Merca, south of Mogadishu, from al-Shabaab. In September, MPs in Mogadishu elect academic and civic activist Hassan Sheikh Mohamud president over the incumbent Sharif Sheikh Ahmed. The first presidential election in Somalia since 1967 follow.

October: African Union and government forces recapture Kismayo, the last major city held by al-Shabaab and the country's second-largest port, and the town of Wanla Weyn, north-west of Mogadishu.

2013

January: The US recognizes Somalia's government for the first time since 1991. In June, veteran al-Shabaab leader, Sheikh Hassan Dahir Aweys, is taken into custody by government troops, after he is ousted by the more extreme al-Shabaab figure Ahmed Abdi Godane. There is a spike in violence, with various attacks by al-Shabaab, including on the presidential palace and UN compound in Mogadishu.

September: Al-Shabaab seize the Westgate shopping centre in the Kenyan capital, Nairobi, killing sixty people, saying it is in retaliation for Kenya's military involvement in Somalia.

2014

May: Al-Shabaab claims responsibility for the bomb attack on a restaurant in Djibouti, saying the country is used as a launch pad to strike at Muslims. In June, al-Shabaab claims responsibility for two attacks on the Kenyan coast, killing more than sixty, saying operations against Kenya would continue. Al-Shabaab leader Ahmed Abdi Godane is killed in a US drone strike in September. The government offers a two-million-dollar bounty on his successor, Ahmad Omar.

November–December: Al-Shabaab carry out mass killings in north-east Kenya, including on a bus and a camp of quarry workers.

2015

April: Al-Shabaab claim responsibility for killing 148 people, mainly Christian students, at the Garissa University College in northern Kenya. The Nairobi government retaliates by carrying out air raids on al-Shabaab bases in Somalia.

2016

February: Government and African Union troops recapture the southern port of Merca that al-Shabaab had briefly seized.

November: The leaders of two Somali states, Puntland and Galmudug, agree to respect a ceasefire in the disputed city of Galkayo. Fighting in the city reportedly displaces 90,000 people.

INTRODUCTION

Few countries in Africa have had such powerful links with both the Soviet Union and the United States – each for years at a stretch – as Somalia, or more correctly, the Federal Republic of Somalia.

From a quiet Indian Ocean backwater that had once been an Italian colony, it remained aloof for a long time from the kind of power struggles that beset other African countries like Ghana, the Congo, Guinea, Algeria, the Sudan and quite a few more in the 1970s.

Overnight, that all changed in 1969, when the Somali army, led by Major General Siad Barre, grabbed power. His first move was to abrogate all security links he might have had with the West and to invite Moscow to become, as he would phrase it, 'my trusted ally'.

Bakaara Market, Mogadishu. (Photo AMISOM Public Information)

The Soviet move was not only unexpected, but it was, as one hack phrased it 'an overnight revolt against all things linked to the West', with Moscow establishing several air bases in the interior while stationing its warships in Somali ports.

Baledogle, a small airport north of Mogadishu, became the biggest Soviet air base in black Africa, from where Soviet military aircraft operated across much of the Indian Ocean. Washington, London, Paris, Riyadh, Jerusalem, Addis Ababa and Nairobi were appalled, but there was little they could do.

An impetuous man, Siad Barre believed his links with the Kremlin were secure enough to realize the Somali imperial ambition of annexing several neighbouring regions. The Somali flag has a five-pointed star, signifying the five regions of 'Greater Somalia', two of which lay in neighbouring countries. One of these was Djibouti, a miniscule former French colony on the Red Sea. The other was Ogaden, which lay to the immediate north in what was formerly known as Abyssinia.

But when he invaded Ethiopia's Ogaden Province – Addis Ababa was then Washington's staunchest friend in Africa's Horn –the Soviets had had enough.

Mogadishu from the air. (Photo ctsnow)

To the consternation of the West, the Kremlin abandoned the Mogadishu government and embraced Addis Ababa.

That resulted in the Russians giving full support in the Ogaden War to the people of Ethiopia, establishing the largest international airlift of weapons since the Six-Day War.

For more than a decade thereafter, conditions within Somalia deteriorated markedly. A number of the country's tribal leaders established themselves as 'warlords', some with Soviet support, others getting succour from Western sources. The country spiralled into anarchy. Conditions became so bad, that in 1992 the United Nations eventually stepped in with Operation Restore Hope, ostensibly intended to help Somalia's starving millions.

Technically an 'invasion', Operation Restore Hope was a multinational force headed by the United States military, created for conducting humanitarian operations in Somalia. The starving masses were only part of the equation.

The move was controversial from the moment the first batch of US Marines stepped ashore on Mogadishu's beaches – in the full glare of waiting television crews whose batteries of lights illuminated the way– with many tribal leaders retaining either clandestine Soviet links or receiving aid from radical Arab forces. Some of these disparate elements included powerful al-Qaeda cadres.

Worse still, it took only a day or two thereafter for several warlords to lay claim to food supplies that started to be unloaded from freighters that berthed in Mogadishu port, the idea being that this largesse would be handed over piecemeal to those desperate people who were worst off, and free of charge.

But there was no controlling the belligerent demagogues. Most of the food aid ended up on the open market, where those in need were expected to pay for whatever was on offer.

The situation soon became intractable. The warlords, having spotted a gap – with the multinational forces of Operation Restore Hope either unable or unwilling to stop the rot   moved into the next phase in a bid to dominate the status quo. Washington, unaccustomed to this kind of strident tribal militancy and in fear of being regarded as politically incorrect, sat back and did nothing.

Although both the United Nations and a powerful African Union (AU) military force continue to maintain a strong presence in the country, a high level of hostilities, as well as multiple killings, continue.

AMISOM forces in Mogadishu. (Photo AMISOM Public Information)

For the record, it is worth looking at how conditions have developed since Operation Restore Hope, together with an insight into some of the previous developments.

Al-Qaeda, through its surrogate insurgent force al-Shabaab, remains a major player in Somalia, receiving its support from Iran, today a close ally of the Russians.

There is still much evidence of the role that the former Soviet air base at Baledogle originally played in Somalia, including scores of jet engines abandoned where they had originally been deposited alongside the main runway. All this sophisticated equipment, abandoned, rusted and useless today, was to have been used to build fighter jets, planned before the Ogaden débâcle.

A new form of post-Soviet terrorism has emerged in Somalia. Suicide bombings have become commonplace, regarded by many because of Iranian and al-Qaeda involvement with al-Shabaab.

Even today, Somali insurgents never dare touch Moscow's interests in the country. The Russians in Somalia are hardly ever molested and, unlike many Western embassies, their diplomatic enclaves are regarded as sacrosanct by the jihadis.

The story begins in 1950, when Italian Somaliland (southern Somalia) became a UN trust territory under Italian administration.

Renamed Somalia six years later, the country was granted internal autonomy and subsequently held its first elections, won by the Somali Youth League. In July 1960, both British and Italian Somaliland were granted independence, uniting to form the independent Republic of Somalia. Aden Abdullah Osman Daar became the first president, but the newly revived country's borders were not clearly defined, resulting in border skirmishes and hostilities with Kenya and Ethiopia throughout the 1960s.

On 15 October 1969, President Shermarke was assassinated by a member of his own police force. Mohamed Siad Barre seized power in the subsequent coup, and in 1970, he declared Somalia a socialist state, strengthening ties with the Soviet Union and subjecting the country to his absurd ideology of 'scientific socialism'.

In 1974, Somalia joined the Arab League, which, with the support of countries like Egypt, Libya, Saudi Arabia and Iraq, should have brought peace. But in 1977–78, Somali forces invaded the Ogaden region of Ethiopia, an area roughly the size of Norway or Malaysia, traditionally inhabited by Somali nomads. It has always been a remote, semi-arid region, with no large cities that has been subject to numerous border hostilities since the 1960s.

The invasion was a gamble. The president did not anticipate the Soviets, their former allies, rushing to help the government of Ethiopia. A major war followed in which thousands were killed on both sides, but, eventually, the better-equipped Ethiopian army and air force prevailed.

Somali troops were forced out by the Soviets and Cubans, prompting Barre to expel his Soviet advisers and strengthen ties with the United States who, until then, had been uncharacteristically relegated to the side lines. Somalia and Ethiopia signed a peace accord in 1988.

In 1991, the recalcitrant Siad Barre was forced out of office. The collapse of his government led to a series of feudal struggles up and down the coast, and, ultimately, to a full-blown civil war. This was followed by the arrival of a United Nations peacekeeping mission, which was to operate in Somalia between 1992 and 1995.

Concurrently, the civil discord that followed the failure of Barre's administration led to a serious humanitarian crisis in Somalia, which prompted further action from the international community, including the arrival of an American-led task force in 1992, named Operation Restore Hope.

AH-1W Cobras
aboard USS *Tripoli*
off Somalia in 1992.
(Photo Joseph Dorey,
US Navy)

The following year, Somali rebels shot down two US helicopters, leading to a battle in which hundreds of Somali citizens were killed.

On 24 September 2001, the UN announced the withdrawal of its entire international staff from Somalia, declaring that it was no longer able to guarantee their safety. The following year, the US announced increased military operations in the country, which it suspected of being an al-Qaeda refuge.

The transitional Federal Somali Government was inaugurated in Kenya – its temporary base– at a conference on 10 October 2004 where Abdullahi Yusuf was elected president. It is worth mentioning that this was the fourteenth attempt to restore some kind of effective central government since 1991, with President Yusuf making an urgent plea to the international community 'to stand by us and help us disarm our militias'. It had little effect, however, because factional differences between the tribes resulted in still more fighting.

In 2005, the transitional government returned from Kenya to Somalia, but divisions remained. Rebels began to hijack food shipments off the coast, leading to the suspension of several aid programmes. On 30 May, rival factions battled for control of Baidoa in south-west Somalia, where Yusuf planned to establish a temporary capital. In November, gunmen attempted to assassinate interim Prime Minister Ali Mohamed Ghedi, attacking his convoy in Mogadishu.

In 2006, Mogadishu experienced the worst violence in more than a decade, as fierce fighting broke out between rival militias.

On 26 February 2006, the transitional government met for the first time on home soil, in Baidoa. That same month, a UN Security Council resolution declared that no neighbouring states should send their forces into Somalia and that only African Union peacekeepers should be involved, but the resolution was ignored by Somalia's old enemy, Ethiopia, which sent the Islamists into retreat.

On 27 December 2006, Ethiopia was urged to withdraw by the African Union and the Arab League. The next day, Mogadishu was recaptured by the government with the help of Ethiopian troops. In January 2007, the transitional government regained control, with President Yusuf entering Mogadishu for the first time since becoming president.

Three months later, the UN authorized an African Union peacekeeping mission. In June 2007, the United States carried out air strikes, the first known American direct military intervention since 1993, targeting al-Qaeda figures in southern Somalia. The following month, in protest, Islamist leaders boycotted a national reconciliation conference in Mogadishu.

The Ethiopian prime minister promised not to withdraw his troops until the 'jihadists' were defeated. Ethiopian, Somali and Islamist forces were accused of war crimes by Human Rights Watch, which claimed the UN Security Council was indifferent to the issues at stake.

The role of the United States in Somalia's internal politics is significant, especially since the country is regarded as one of the most important revolutionary staging areas in Africa and the Middle East. Al-Qaeda – and its al-Shabaab jihadi counterpart – maintains numerous peripatetic bases in Somalia. While always on the move for security reasons, these bases increasingly come under attack, not only by US special forces units, but also by remotely piloted vehicles (RPVs) launched from neighbouring Djibouti, a former French colony on the Red Sea.

America's Combined Joint Task Force–Horn of Africa (CJTF-HOA) was established some years ago in Djibouti's Camp Lemonnier. Formerly the headquarters of the French Foreign Legion, for a long time it served as the focal point for Washington's Department of Defense efforts in the region. For security reasons, that headquarters has since been moved into Djibouti's remote interior, to an area immediately south of the Danakil Depression.

Mogadishu airport during the American invasion. Note the freight plane approaching from the right (Photo Al J. Venter)

Notably, CJTF falls under the jurisdiction of the United States Central Command (USCENTCOM).

On average, the staff of the CJTF numbers around 250, and the assigned troops number between 1,200 and 1,800. The US Navy also uses Djibouti to launch surveillance missions in the Red Sea.

The 'combined' aspect of the CJTF is at the staff level only; there are no non-American troops assigned to the US command.

The CJTF-HOA's publicly stated mission is to engage in 'joint and combined training and operations in the CJOA-HOA and AOI to enable Regional Nations to defeat al-Qaeda and Associated Movements (AQAM) and to obtain coalition support to diminish underlying conditions that terrorists seek to exploit and to prevent the re-emergence of AQAM'.

1. EARLY PERIOD

History World's website[1] covers in great detail much of what went before in a series of several thousand narratives and timelines, running from Aegean civilization to Zoroastrianism and gives us a detailed backdrop of early and more recent Somali events. Written by Bamber Gascoigne, he tells us that the land of the Somali people, much of it arid and inhospitable, has for thousands of years been close to civilization and international trade. To the north, just across the Gulf of Aden, is Saba, the land of the legendary Queen of Sheba and the earliest part of Arabia to prosper. To the west is Ethiopia, where the kingdom of Aksum was established by the 5th century BC.

Gascoigne goes on to explain that Somalia's harbours, situated on the Horn of Africa, jutting out into the India Ocean, were natural ports of call for traders sailing to and from India. 'So the coastline of the region was much visited by foreigners, in particular Arabs and Persians and later, by Chinese explorers. But in the arid interior the Somali people were left to their own devices.'

Enter other European powers, including France and Italy, with both nations having established settlements in the north, adjacent to the Red Sea, the former establishing a permanent base in what was to eventually become the Republic of Djibouti in 1977 and Italy taking control of much of the south. Britain made claims of its own in an expansive desert region that was listed as Somaliland on the charts up to the mid-20th century. This region has since hived off into a form of unrecognized semi-autonomy, refusing to acknowledge the authority of the Mogadishu government. Like Puntland, to its immediate south-east, contemporary Somaliland regards the central government as unable to control its own affairs.

More than a century before, undeterred by the strong European presence, Abyssinian Emperor Menelik II also laid claim to vast regions along his southern fringes, with a large part of it – Ogaden – in dispute for almost a century. Earlier, Gascoigne writes, 'Italy had established protectorates along the coast eastwards beyond British Somaliland while Italian companies acquired leases on parts of the east-facing Somali coast (where the landlord was the sultan of Zanzibar). Italy agreed spheres of influence amicably with Britain in 1884, placing the border between British Somaliland and Italian

Somalia just west of Bender Cassim … At first Italy was on congenial terms with Ethiopia, notably in the 1889 treaty of Uccialli concerning Eritrea. But disagreement over the actual meaning of the Eritrean treaty rapidly soured. By 1896 this resulted in outright war and in the crushing defeat of the Italians at Adwa, an event still celebrated annually throughout Ethiopia.' At the time this was the greatest defeat inflicted on a European army since the age of Hannibal and its consequences were felt well into the 20th century. History World maintains, 'As an example of colonial warfare on an epic scale, it cannot be surpassed.'

The first real uprising against colonialism occurred when Somalis sought to push the Ethiopians out of the Ogaden region but this uprising – largely tribal in context – then expanded to target European colonists as well. The Dervish State, headed by Mohammed Abdille Hassan, an Ogaden himself whom the British referred to as 'Mad Mullah', conducted a religious-based war of resistance against the Ethiopians and British from 1899 to 1920 when he was eventually defeated. The war resulted in the death of nearly a third of northern Somalia's population.

Italy's presence in the Horn became more pronounced over the years and culminated with fascist Benito Mussolini hoping to expand his interests across a vast swathe of Africa that stretched from Libya on the Mediterranean all the way south through the Sudan to the Indian Ocean. Egypt also came into the equation but Mussolini had not reckoned on the British being so resolute. A new era of conflict had begun in Somalia in 1923 with the arrival in the Italian colony of the first governor appointed by the fascist government in Rome. Mussolini had already made Africa a colonial priority, his intent clearly to follow in the footsteps of what France and Britain had achieved in West and Central Africa, and Germany in what are today Namibia, Tanzania and the Cameroons before being forced out of Africa after the First World War. One of his first moves was to sign the Treaty of Lausanne, which formalized Italy's still-disputed administration of Libya.

Having been able to entrench his administrative presence in Somalia, Mussolini's next step was to try to force Abyssinia into making aggressive moves towards his possessions along the coast, especially since Emperor Haile Selassie was in search of a suitable harbour that the landlocked country had been denied in Europe's 'African Scramble'. Both France and Italy controlled Ethiopia's only possible approaches to the Red Sea. But the wise old

Mussolini and Hitler
in Munich, June 1940.
(Photo Eva Braun)

fox, Haile Selassie, acutely aware of Mussolini's colonial aspirations would not be prompted into taking any kind of action that might be construed by the Italians as aggressive.

That impasse resulted in Mussolini invading Ethiopia in October 1935 and thus launching the Second Italo-Abyssinian War. Haile Selassie's forces fought bravely, but they could not counter the modern weapons fielded by the Italians, many of which had come from Nazi Germany, then also preparing for involvement in a foreign conflict, the Spanish Civil War.

Seven months after hostilities began Emperor Haile Selassie fled the country and Mussolini's forces moved into the interior and took the capital, Addis Ababa.

In the interim, the Italians dedicated significant effort towards developing their twin East African colonies of Eritrea and Somalia by making their respective capitals Mogadishu and Berbera into fairly modern African cities where the Italian expatriate communities would be thoroughly at home. In fact, they were hugely successful, having initiated many of the facilities enjoyed by Italians in Europe – good hotels, a network of roads reaching into the interior, reliable communications, and health and banking systems. Both colonies attracted thousands of permanent settlers. In fact, when this author visited Mogadishu in the late 1960s and 1970s, he found the Somali capital one of the most pleasant 'ports of call' along the entire East African coast.

Whitehall, in contrast, took a more hands-off approach to governance of its portion of the Somali peninsula, leaving more responsibility in the hands of local leaders but also providing less by way of infrastructure. These distinctions are often cited as underpinnings of the incompatibility that would arise between the various colonial regions, of which Abyssinia, soon to be renamed Ethiopia, was a vital cog.

This colonial history, in addition to other dynamics, is also seen to play a role in the subsequent contrasting levels of stability of Somalia and Somaliland. During the Second World War, the entire East African region became an immediate focus of attention, Mussolini having signed up to the 'Axis of Evil'.

On the outbreak of the Second World War, the Duke of Aosta, the viceroy of Italian East Africa (Africa Orientale Italiana), had between 250,000 and 280,000 Italian troops on hand to maintain power. By 10 June 1940, the Italians were organized into four command sectors: the Northern Sector (Asmara, Eritrea), Southern Sector (Jimma, Ethiopia), Eastern Sector (near the border with French Somaliland and British Somaliland), as well as the Giuba Sector in the south (Kismayu). Lieutenant-General Luigi Frusci commanded the Northern Sector, General Pietro Gazzera the Southern Sector, General Guglielmo Nasi the Eastern Sector and Lieutenant-General Carlo de Simone the Giuba Sector. The Duke of Aosta maintained overall command from Addis Ababa.

Most of the Italian troops in East Africa – almost three-quarters of the entire force – were local East African *askari*. While native troops of the regular Eritrean battalions and the Somali colonial troops of the Regio Corpo Truppe Coloniali (Royal Corps of Colonial Troops) were among the best Italian units in East Africa, the majority of the colonial troops in Italian East Africa were recruited, trained and equipped to do little more than maintain order in the colony. The Somali *dubats* (literally 'white turbans'), recruited from border clansmen, provided useful light infantry and skirmishers but the irregular *bande* were much less effective. Ethiopian *askari* and irregulars, recruited during the brief Italian occupation, deserted in large numbers after the outbreak of war. The Royal Corps of Colonial Troops included horse-mounted Eritrean cavalry known as 'Falcon Feathers' (*Penne di Falco*). A squadron of these horsemen once charged a large section of Commonwealth troops, rather ineffectively hurling hand grenades from the saddle.

Once South African General Smuts had entered the war against the Axis powers, an immediate effort was made to send several large units north by road from South Africa to Kenya. More South African forces came in by sea from Durban. It was the second time that South Africa had mobilized its people to support its old Boer War enemy against the Germans and their allies.

To appreciate the problems facing the Allies, the topography of Kenya itself must be considered, as it had to be traversed to get to Somalia and dictated the lines on which the services, especially the engineers, transport companies and field ambulances, would have to develop and operate. The frontier of Kenya and Italian East Africa stretched for 2,000 kilometres from Lake Rudolf to the Indian Ocean, between Lamu and Kismayu, at points well over 50 kilometres in depth, and across almost its entire length it ran through arid bush and semi-desert, except briefly where it crossed a rocky but green escarpment at Moyale.

Three South African Air Force squadrons, including outdated Hawker Hartebeest fighters, were sent to Kenya during the first few months of 1940 and when South Africa declared war against Rome on 11 June, these units immediately attacked Italian positions, air and ground forces, petrol and ammunition dumps and lines of communication in an effort to offset the Regia Aeronautica's numerical superiority in the air. The intent was to prevent Italian land forces from gaining further ground. The first South African infantry and support units arrived in Mombasa, Kenya, in early June. By the end

Italian-era Somali *askari*.

Italian troops at Moyale in East Africa, shortly before being overrun by the South African Army, 1941.

of July, the 1st South African Infantry Brigade Group had arrived and weeks later the 1st South African Division was formed. This division included the 1st, 2nd, and 5th infantry brigade groups.

By the end of the year, there were 27,000 South Africans serving in East Africa, either in the 1st South African Division, the 11th African Division or 12th African Division. Each South African brigade group consisted of three rifle battalions, an armoured car company, and supporting signal, engineer, and medical units.

The assault by the South African 2nd and 5th infantry brigades together with the East African 25th Infantry Brigade on the enemy in southern Abyssinia was highly successful and in February 1941 the fort at Hobuk and the fortress of Mega fell to the Allies.

Meantime the South Africans, joined by a battalion of troops from the Gold Coast (Ghana today), defeated the enemy at El Wak on the Kenyan–Somaliland border from where they moved on to Kismayu on the coast. After crossing the Juba River, the Allies moved forward in strength to Mogadishu which was captured on 24 February 1941.

With the Italian resistance in Somaliland eliminated, British General Cunningham decided to immediately strike north from Mogadishu, following the Italian-built Strada Imperiale across the barren plains of north-eastern Abyssinia towards Jijiga and Harar, the latter being the country's second-most important city. The distance of about 1,200 kilometres was covered in seventeen days countering Italian resistance all the way. After fierce fighting in the vicinity of Harar and Dire Dawa (a major Italian air base), the Allied troops reached the Awash River on 2 April 1941. Four days later, again with the South Africans in the van, they captured the Abyssinian capital Addis Ababa unopposed.

The war was not yet over. After their defeat by General Platt at the Battle of Keren, the remnants of the Italian Eritrean army had fallen back to the southeast towards Dessie and Amba Alagi to link up with the defeated armies fleeing north from Addis Ababa.

In the interim, the Emperor of Abyssinia, Haile Selassie, in exile in Britain since 1936, had returned to his country via the Sudan and collected a motley army of brigands and rebels, called the Shifta, which was now also marching on Addis Ababa and the Italian strongholds at Amba Alagi and Gondar. The two fiercest battles the South Africans would fight during the entire campaign were in the mountain maze of Dessie and Amba Alagi north of Addis Ababa. Towering 3,000 metres into the sky, the peak of Amba Alagi was surrounded by a jumble of mountains and ravines which, in May 1941, were enveloped by biting winds, rain, mist and sleet. On 18 May 1941, after fifteen days of tenacious assault by British, Indian and South African troops, the Duke of Aosta, Commander-in-Chief of the Italian East African Army, formally surrendered. The rainy season postponed the final reduction of some Italian garrisons which had taken refuge in ancient forts in the mountain country of northwest Abyssinia, but, on 27 November 1941, General Nasi, the last of the Italian commanders in the field, surrendered the fortress at Gondar.[2] The East Africa Campaign was over.

Britain was to rule these territories as military protectorates until 1949, at which time the newly formed United Nations granted Italy a trusteeship over most of present-day Somalia. The British maintained the trusteeship over what is today the self-declared state of Somaliland. Bamber Gascoigne: 'Between 1948 and 1950 the situation reverted to the colonial boundaries agreed in 1897. Ethiopia retained the Ogaden and the Haud. French and British Somaliland continued as before. In 1950 the Italians returned to Somalia under a UN trusteeship, with the commitment to bring the colony to independence within ten years.'

After the ten-year interim period, on 26 June 1960, the northern protectorate of Somaliland gained independence from Britain. Five days later, on 1 July 1960, the two former colonies united to form the United Republic of Somalia under President Aden Abdullah Osman Daar, Prime Minister Abdirashid Ali Shermarke and a 123-member National Assembly representing both territories. Daar ruled Somalia from 1960 until 1967. Shermarke succeeded him and led the country for two years until his assassination in 1969. Though northern and southern Somalia were united under one government, they operated as two separate countries, with different legal, administrative and educational systems. On the day of Shermarke's funeral, the Somali army, led by Mohamed Siad Barre, staged a bloodless coup.[3]

Barre, a charismatic but utterly ruthless military man who fostered a cult of personality and called himself 'Victorious Leader', served as president and military ruler of Somalia from 1969–1991 and renamed the country the Somali Democratic Republic. Under Barre's brutal leadership Somalia sided with the Soviet Union in the Cold War and while he proscribed tribalism and promoted his own 'Scientific Socialism', he supported clan chieftains in maintaining control of rural areas. The new government, dominated by the only legal political party, the Supreme Revolutionary Council, or SRC, formed a guiding ideology based on a combination of Marxism and the Quran and led a 're-education' campaign to eliminate opposition. In 1976 the SRC officially marked the end of military rule by dissolving itself and ceding power to its own creation, the Somali Revolutionary Socialist Party, or SRSP.[4]

During these developments, a major recurring political theme in independent Somalia was the need to reunite with three large Somali groups 'trapped', as Mogadishu maintained, in other states. The three 'offshoots' were in French Somaliland, in Ethiopia (the annexed Ogaden and Haud regions) as well as in northern Kenya. Failure to make any progress on this issue was largely due to western support for Ethiopia and Kenya, which caused Somalia to look to the Soviet Union for military aid. Nevertheless the Somali government managed

Soldiers of the King's African Rifles during the British advance into Italian Somaliland, February 1941. (Photo H.J. Clements)

to maintain a fairly neutral stance in international affairs during the 1960s, a position which changed dramatically after 1969.

In 1977, with Ethiopia in chaos after the fall of Emperor Haile Selassie, Somalia attacked Ethiopian garrisons in the Ogaden. But President Siad was betrayed by the Soviet Union who regarded Ethiopia as a more important potential client. Early in 1978 the Ethiopian army, deploying Soviet equipment and reinforced by troops from Cuba, recaptured the Ogaden. The result was the mass exodus of hundreds of thousands of Somali refugees over the borders into Somalia. In the aftermath of this disaster, clan-based guerrilla groups were

Left: Visit of Emperor Haile Selassie of Ethiopia on the USS *Quincy* in the Great Bitter Lake, Egypt, February 1945. (Photo US National Archives and Records Administration)

Below: British forces demolish fascist stone monument, Kismayo, Italian Somaliland, 1941. (Photo H.J. Clements)

formed in and around Somalia with the intention of toppling Siad's repressive centralist regime. By 1988 the country was in the grips of a full-scale civil war, resulting in the overthrow of the tyrant Siad in 1991.

The conflict destroyed Somalia's crops during 1992 and brought widespread famine. Food flown in by international agencies was looted by the warring militias. By December 1992 the situation caused the UN to actively intervene, sending a force of 35,000 troops into the country under the auspices of Operation Restore Hope. The UN briefly calmed the situation, persuading fifteen warring groups to convene in Addis Ababa in January 1993 for peace and disarmament talks. These seemed at first to make progress, but the situation continued to deteriorate. In March 1994 American and European units in the UN force withdrew, finding the level of casualties unacceptable. Troops from African countries and the Indian subcontinent remained *in situ.*

During the rest of the decade the situation deteriorated still further. From late 1994 Mogadishu, was divided between the two most powerful warring factions, with the respective leaders of each declaring themselves president. In March 1995 remaining UN forces were evacuated from the coast under the protection of an international flotilla. At the end of the decade the only remotely stable region was the breakaway republic of Somaliland, in the north-west. An interim constitution was introduced there in 1997 and a president elected. But the would-be republic failed to win any international recognition.

In a messy litany of tribalism, colonialism, world wars and cold war, the 20th century came to a violent close with Somalia consigned to essentially 'non-state' status, ungoverned and ungovernable, with industrial-scale humanitarian disasters befalling the territory on a regular basis. The 21st century would usher in further turmoil and bloodshed as Islamist colonizers in the guise of al-Qaeda and al-Shabaab sought to stamp their footprint across the region.

2. NIGHT MISSION TO MOGADISHU

Eastern Exit Chronology

5 December 1990: Ambassador Bishop recommends the voluntary departure of all non-essential US personnel.

19 December: Number of official US personnel reduced from 147 to 37.

30 December: Full-scale fighting between Somali government and rebel forces breaks out in Mogadishu.

1 January 1991: US Ambassador requests authority to evacuate embassy.

2 January: Ambassador Bishop requests military assistance for evacuation; the USS *Guam* and USS *Trenton* get under way at 11.30 pm local time.

4 January: Gun battle between US embassy personnel and looters; Italian and Soviet attempts to evacuate via fixed-wing aircraft fail.

5 January: CH-53Es launched from *Guam* 466 nautical miles from Mogadishu, insert a 60-man evacuation force and return to *Guam* with 61 evacuees aboard.

6 January: Four waves of CFI-46s evacuate the remaining 220 evacuees and the 60-man evacuation force in the early morning. Mission declared complete.

10 January: Baby born on board the *Guam* in early morning.

11 January: Evacuees disembark at the Omani port of Muscat.

While the eyes of the world focused, seemingly mesmerized, on Operation Desert Shield and the Persian Gulf, a modest US Marine and Navy SEAL force staged a daring and flawless night rescue of 250 American citizens and foreign nationals from an embattled Mogadishu, Somalia, early in January 1991.

USS *Guam.*
(Photo US Navy)

Captain Robert Doss, a United States Marine mission planner and Boeing Vertol CH-46E Sea Knight 'Phrog' helicopter pilot with HMM-263 (helicopter medium marine) Squadron during Operation Eastern Exit – for that is what the rescue mission was called – takes up the story, with R.R. Keene of the Marine Corps Association and Foundation filling in gaps.

The arrival of 1991 found Amphibious Group Two and the 4th Marine Expeditionary Brigade wrapping up their fourth month in the Middle East. The USS *Guam* (LPH-9), with Marine Medium Helicopter Squadrons (HMM) 263 and 365, and elements of 1st Battalion, 2nd Marine Regiment, left the Persian Gulf to conduct night-vision goggle (NVG) training and support Maritime Interdiction Force operations in the North Arabian Sea.

A detachment of HMM-263 helicopters on board the USS *Trenton* (LPD-14) had shortly before intercepted two defiant Iraqi vessels, the *Ibn Khaldoon* and the *Ain Zalah*, for the UN-sanctioned boarding and inspection by an embarked naval raid force.

President George Bush's 15 January deadline for the Iraqi withdrawal from Kuwait loomed ominously. We remained uncertain that the Gulf War would begin in two weeks, even as we continued to prepare intensely for it. Our force, literally, had issued arctic gear for a NATO deployment on one August day, replaced it with desert camouflage the next, then departed for the Middle

East a few days later. For the Marines in the Brigade responding to these rapidly changing events, the words 'every clime and place' from the Marines Hymn rang true.

Rumours always find a home on board ship, and, as day turned into night on 2 January, a new bit of 'scuttlebutt' started about trouble in Somalia. The country was being torn apart by a brutal civil war that ravaged the capital city of Mogadishu.

The US embassy there was under a furious challenge, as rebels and government forces roamed the streets outside, leaving a wake of terror and indiscriminate death and violence.

When our aircraft were recalled to the ship that evening, we learned we were headed to Somalia to conduct a 'non-combatant evacuation operation' to rescue Americans and foreign nationals from the US embassy compound, which lies to the immediate north of Mogadishu Airport. We were told that other navies, air forces, and commercial carriers had attempted evacuations, but the fighting drove them away.

As the amphibious assault ship *Guam* and the amphibious transport dock *Trenton* (LPD-14) started south, information about the threat, evacuees, and

US diplomatic compound, Mogadishu, target area of the rescue effort. (Photo Al J. Venter)

landing zones had not yet begun to arrive; no one knew the exact location of the embassy compound and, of course, there were no adequate maps.

The first word we received from the US Ambassador in Somalia, James Bishop, detailed the desperate situation there. Each message provided a small piece of the planning puzzle, but kept us wondering if we were doing enough. More important, were we doing it in time?

Mission-planning cells worked feverishly to construct a plan for the evacuation. Fortunately, problems with communication and coordination never materialized; aviation, ground, and Navy units on the *Guam* had developed a rapport in the preceding months that supported close cooperation.

Incoming communication from the US Embassy gave some of us the distinct impression that they were being written from cover, beneath a desk as a fire-fight raged nearby; one message reported that a rocket-propelled grenade had slammed into the compound; others described automatic-weapons fire and armed aggressors being repulsed as they scaled the walls of the compound.

The ships were making best speed southwards out of the Persian Gulf, but despite the intensity with which we planned, we could not forestall those who threatened our embassy and diplomats. Our course paralleled the coast of Somalia, a lengthy stretch of shoreline just north of Kenya that leads to Mogadishu.

In the very early hours of 5 January, following another frantic call from Ambassador Bishop, we moved to within the range of our CH-53E Sea Stallion helicopters, with their aerial refuelling capability. The most recent messages from the embassy indicated that the compound was in imminent danger of being overrun – with the logical implication to all of us that the evacuation effort would be lost as well.

Two giant Sea Stallions from Marine Heavy Helicopter Squadron 461 on board the *Trenton* were loaded with troops and sent on a 466-mile overwater night flight to reinforce the compound and assist with the evacuation: Operation Eastern Exit was begun. Supporting them were a pair of Two Marine KC-130 turbo-prop tankers out of Bahrain to provide fuel for the ultra-thirsty, troop-laden Super Stallions.

The flight was not without event. During the first refuelling a pressure seal on the second CH-53E failed. Fuel apparently sprayed into the cabin but the leak was quickly fixed by the crew chief and refuelling continued.

USS *Trenton.* (Photo Ola K. Sanders)

Also, because the choppers' Omega Navigation Systems were not functioning properly, the pilots had to rely on the refuelling C-130s as well as directional control from the ships.

Altogether a 60-man Marine evacuation force, including a nine-man SEAL team was landed in the embassy compound, supplementing the five Marine security guards who had been 'holding the fort' until then. They were a most welcome addition to the team.

Earlier that morning, State Department officials were reporting that the street outside was '. . . littered with corpses, looters had been repulsed with small-arms fire by hired security guards,' and 'an embassy building had sustained a direct hit from a rocket-propelled grenade'.

Their 'run-in' was not without event. Because of the lack of adequate maps, the CH-53Es spent 20 minutes meandering over Mogadishu in the dark looking for the embassy compound. They found it eventually, but it was a close-run thing.

Meanwhile, US Marine security guards in the embassy, playing their traditional role, were responsible for the destruction of sensitive and classified material, cryptographic and communications equipment, and protection of the embassy building itself. They also assisted in providing radio communications and helping with evacuation preparations.

Quite often they would be called to give fire-support to the contracted Somali guards who manned posts at the perimeter of the compound and who, according to the State Department, repulsed looters. Some of these insurgents arrived with scaling ladders for the three-metre -high walls.

State Department officials also confirmed that American officials in Mogadishu, at the request of officials at the Soviet embassy in Washington and the Foreign Ministry in Moscow, had arranged to evacuate all Soviet personnel from their embassy in the Somali capital. The Soviet ambassador, his staff and their dependents were escorted several kilometres to the US Embassy by troops loyal to President Barre.

Indeed, 141 men, 72 women and 47 children (including the new-born daughter of the Sudanese ambassador) from 30 nationalities and various legations within the city had fled to sanctuary offered by the 80-acre compound.

Once arrived, the new US Marine contingents poured from the Super Stallions to reinforce and take up defensive positions beside the Somali

US Marine Corps CH-53E Sea Stallion landing on the amphibious dock landing ship USS *Harpers Ferry*. (Photo Joshua J. Wahl)

guards. Others were dispatched and made a dash of two blocks to the US Office of Military Cooperation to escort several Americans and the Kenyan ambassador, who had been cut off by crossfire between warring factions to the embassy.

For all this, the first of the evacuees had been gathered together, loaded on board and ferried to the safety of the *Guam*, still more than 300 miles and another aerial refuelling away. Italian C-130s had tried another evacuation effort at the airport, but increasingly bitter fighting kept them from returning to Mogadishu that day.

A flight of Italian C-130s marked with red crosses did manage to land later at the airport and a French frigate – also redirected from Desert Shield – managed to get close enough to the Somali coast to pick up 47 people near Merca, about 70 kilometres south of Mogadishu.

Mission planning on board the *Guam* continued. The timing of the main evacuation was a key concern as the team also considered the possibility of a daylight mission with the option of a night alternative.

Daylight, it was felt, would afford the Americans with the opportunity for an evenly paced, hands-above-the-table evacuation. If their helicopters might be regarded as an innocuous 'neutral' third party attempting an overt evacuation of innocents by their 'warlord' adversaries, they might possibly proceed unmolested, but there was no guarantee that that could happen.

What raised that possibility initially was that the fact that embassy would be easy to find in daylight: considerably better than trying to spot it in the dark, particularly since the marine pilots had only recently obtained a few black-and-white photographs and 1:50,000 scale maps of the area for navigation purposes.

We were also worried our presence over Mogadishu, day or night, might be construed as a sneak attack on behalf of one or other of the civil war adversaries.

Night-vision goggles would permit us to see in the dark, and we could turn off all of our aircraft lights and become 'invisible' to those on the ground, depriving hostile forces of much of their precision. Nevertheless, any advantage gained by flying in the dark would be lost by overflights looking for a darkened landing zone over extremely hostile positions who, we'd already been told by intelligence sources, had unlimited supplies of ammunition.

To make matters worse, the LZ was described as extremely sandy and filled with unspecified obstacles; even in the daylight, landing five helicopters in such a confined area would be a challenge.

More messages continued to arrive describing further mayhem and conflict around the perimeter of the embassy compound.

The erratic nature of these attacks convinced us that our helicopters would almost certainly be targeted if spotted. With reports that suggested that fighting decreased during the dark hours, the decision was made: we would go in during the night.

It is axiomatic that a night operation poses more dangers than any daytime mission. But these were problems over which pilots could exercise control. That was another factor: at this point, our night option made better tactical sense, simply because we were a force that presumed a capability to strike at night against Iraq. Consequently, there was no reason to balk at a night strike into Somalia.

At 23h30 on 5 January, the first of our two waves of five armed CH-46s, led by aviation mission commander Lieutenant Colonel R.J. Wallace, prepared to launch from 30 miles at sea. We were now close to the capital.

Once in the air, Mogadishu was easy to see through our night-vision goggles. The sky at sea was clear, though the city, itself, was overcast. A pall of smoke drifted to seaward.

It surprised us that Mogadishu still had electrical power. Occasionally we could see flashes of battle and the occasional line of tracers, but not much more. The Initial Point (IP) – the point at which the flight intended to cross the coast – would not be easy to find, but the importance of flying over it on the first crossing had been stressed during planning and briefing.

An error of a thousand metres to the right would take the flight directly over known surface-to-air missile (SAM) and anti-aircraft artillery sites (and presumably troop concentrations). A thousand metres to the left would head us off the edge of our maps. They were the only ones we had, so the initial effort was crucial to the success of the whole operation.

The flight crossed the IP as planned and descended to 100 feet. We slowed down to about 80 knots. Lieutenant Colonel Wallace spotted the embassy compound's infrared strobe light that marked the LZ and transitioned to land.

The decision to put a little distance between aircraft during this final transition proved critical; the LZ was more confined than anticipated and each helicopter 'browned-out' in the whirling sand and debris swept up by the rotors just prior to touch-down.

When the dust settled, we were presented with a view of what it was all about; through our NVGs, we could see groups of civilians huddled near an

CH-46E Sea Knight helicopters conducting flight operations, USS *Bonhomme Richard*. (Photo US Navy)

embassy building. The evacuees moved quickly in organized groups of 15 to board the helicopters. Once seated, the helicopters launched and signalled the second wave of five to begin its ingress.

Like ships, almost, our choppers passed each other in the night – five Thunder aircraft from HMM-263 returning to the ship and five Rugby aircraft from HMM-365 inbound to Mogadishu. Continuing the process, Rugby departed the embassy with evacuees and Thunder prepared to launch from the ship and return to the city.

Suddenly, the silence of the radios was broken by a call from the ambassador's office saying we'd been ordered to cease the evacuation immediately. We were told to leave Somalia or be shot down. Some of us were surprised it had taken the Somalis so long to react.

Since we had begun our operation – with the understanding that the environment was hostile – the threat had no effect on our mission. Crews did however double-check their body armour, and there were some hasty discussions reiterating procedures for the transfer of flight controls between pilots if one of them was hit. There were also rules of engagement passed on to the gunners.

Moments after Thunder's departure from the ship, the overhead Air Force AC-130 reported that his radar warning receiver had detected an active SAM system to the west. Message noted by all of us.

We continued to the embassy and were aware that the situation could only get worse if we delayed the outcome any longer. Approaching the LZ, this time, we received SAM radar-search indications from the east, but by flying low and keeping our airspeeds high, we prevented acquisition and lock-on possibility.

The evacuations continued. One more load for Thunder and another for Rugby. As the number of evacuees dwindled, the security force began to pull inward into a tighter security perimeter in the embassy compound. At this point, as reported by Adam Siegel in *Proceedings: US Naval Institute*, there were some curious developments.

As the second wave arrived, a more serious threat emerged. A Somali major approached the gate with two truckloads of troops and threatened to shoot down the helicopters if the 'illegal operation' did not cease immediately.

With the concurrence of the US Ambassador, the operation continued unimpeded as Ambassador Bishop negotiated with the major.

Because the ambassador, his immediate staff, and the Marine security guards had been scheduled to go on the third wave, it took off for the *Guam* with only a portion of the planned evacuees (and only four helicopters instead of five).

Before the arrival of the final wave, the Somali major withdrew his opposition in exchange for several thousand dollars in cash and the keys to the ambassador's car. The last wave, therefore, had six helicopters.

Final head counts were taken and the last helicopter prepared to leave the LZ. Armed guards massed at the embassy gate and our gunners were prepared to repel and attack, but none materialized. When we were certain no evacuees remained, the last aircraft left.

Meanwhile, reports from Mogadishu were coming in that once the last of the helicopters departed, the American Embassy was sacked and looted by retreating members of Somalia's armed forces who used rocket-propelled grenades to blast down the gate to the compound and doors to the embassy.

On board *Trenton* and *Guam*, evacuees were cared for until they arrived in Muscat, Oman, several days later, where arrangements for return to their home countries were made.

AC-130A gunship.
(Photo Bill Thompson)

CH-46s launching from USS *Guam*. (Photo US Navy)

In the aftermath of that unusual series of events, some astonishing facts emerged, drawn from the reality that Operation Eastern Exit had provided. Navy and Marine commanders on the scene had only had a few hours to come up with a viable plan to evacuate the embassy. So invaluable were the lessons learned that SOC training would include a rapid-planning sequence where US Marines and the United States Navy operated in tandem with each other's assets.

As Lieutenant General Joseph P. Hoar, Marine Corps Deputy Chief of Staff for Plans, Policies and Operations commented, 'Everyone knew what had to be done. It was only 24 hours from the time the first group of helicopters lifted off the *Trenton* until Ambassador Bishop declared the NEO complete.

'Not a shot was fired at or by Marines. Not a person in the evacuation was injured ... in and out and it was over. Bang. Done!'

3. WARS OF NO CONSEQUENCE

Somalia's problems are long-standing and date back almost half a century, and there is little evidence that things are going to change. In fact, with al-Qaeda becoming part of the equation with its surrogate al-Shabaab, and Kenya wishing to send all Somali refugees back to where they came from, conditions can only deteriorate further. The country has been the source of a series of terror attacks in East Africa that have left many innocents dead or maimed. Yet long before General Farrah Aideed or Mogadishu had become a regular source of unsettling news, a drama of horrific proportions was unravelling.

Even by post-imperial African standards, Somalia is a mess. But that's nothing new. The Horn of Africa has been a scarecrow-poor battleground for as long as it has been inhabited by man.

I had been going there from the late 1960s. The first time I flew into Mogadishu was the morning after Armstrong had taken his notorious 'giant step for mankind'. I returned with my wife in the mid-1970s. She found it an interesting experience, but she was also pleased to return to Nairobi after a week. Most Westerners who visit Mogadishu tend to react that way.

In those days, the few journalists who took the trouble to travel to Mogadishu from Addis Ababa (usually on their own initiative after hearing what others were doing in those far-flung spots, and managing to persuade their editors that the country might be newsworthy) found themselves in a totally different environment to anything else they had experienced in Africa.

In fact, before the troubles started, we found a country where little had either happened or changed since British and the South African forces drove the Italians out in 1941. We found people just as surly and antagonistic, which might be expected when there is no work – little prospect of any either. Vehicles on Mogadishu's pitted streets are decrepit, often with twelve-year-olds at the wheel. Electricity supply is erratic, plumbing is capricious, especially in the few hotels still open and that have loos that could actually flush. As the late Bill Deeds once said about the place, it 'was an uncovenanted mercy'.

The main post office in those days had a single bulb in its cavernous roof and the structure boasted no doors or windows. The shutters were lowered when the official felt like it or when the daily shipment of qat arrived from the airport, which was not all that surprising since half the nation was – and still is – addicted.

Mogadishu then had a single public telephone for all public communications with the world outside, cemented onto a concrete pillar in the middle of the hall so that nobody would carry it away. We stood in a reasonably well-ordered single file waiting to make our calls, often far into the night.

Mogadishu, built solidly on a range of white sandstone cliffs that stretches back into the desert behind, was a very different sort of place in the late 1960s. The city, about half the size of Nairobi, is expansive, facing a broad lagoon bounded by a reef several hundred metres out that stretches all the way up and down this part of the Indian Ocean coast.

It was a little like one of those tiny colonial outposts that we read about at school, Pago Pago in the Pacific, or Mahé in the Seychelles before that country built its first airport and international tourism took over. Mogadishu then was safe, at least before the jihadis arrived. Then, as my wife and I discovered, we could sleep securely without worrying that somebody might lob a grenade through our open window or try to force the door and slash our throats.

Approaching Mogadishu Airport in a US Army Black Hawk (Photo Al J. Venter)

Nobody stole anything from our hotel room, such as it was, and twice my wife had to walk a kilometre or more in the dark to the post office to call home. She was never molested or insulted in those mysterious, malodorous streets.

Before war levelled the town, the Italian imprint was ubiquitous. There were raffia-clad bottles of Chianti on every dinner table, the chemist's shop bearing the legend *Farmacia* was manned by knowledgeable expatriates, and the police wore the kind of peaked caps issued under the rule of the dictator Mussolini with the same-style cap badges of Fascismo Italiano.

Indeed, in the 1960s and 1970s, Mogadishu reflected a dilapidated sun-bleached mixture of European, African and Muslim buildings, some with high walls and steel gates enclosing tropical gardens that were a delight. It was a bit like parts of the Côte d'Azur, only all the faces were dark and the inhabitants wore the kind of garb that Somalis like – long, easy-flowing robes from which the East African *kikoi* or *kitenge* were adapted.

At the heart of the city stood a magnificent Roman Catholic cathedral, the biggest, it was said, south of the Mediterranean, but like much else in the capital, it was gutted during the civil war. There was also a fine old imperial arch in the colonial Italian tradition, complete with marble columns enriched with bas-reliefs. Modelled in the fashion of the great Roman period, fundamentalist Muslim revolutionaries who took the city over decided early on that it had to go. So, word has it, they blasted it with dynamite.

Il Villaggio Anzilotti was the suburb where the best brothels were to be found, west of the old harbour that Gaius Plinius Secundus – Pliny the Elder – mentioned in his writings almost 2,000 years ago. The streets were all *viae* – Via Damasco, Via Roma, Via Congo and so on. It is quite an ancient place and perhaps the oldest permanent Islamic settlement on the east coast of Africa south of the Sudan.

Towards dusk, we foreign waifs would drift along 'sunset strip' towards a succession of diplomatic beach clubs that stood in neat rows, each commanding its own few square metres of yellow sand by the lagoon. The British encampment was next to the Russian one, or was it the Polish? Alongside that stood the American 'home from home', the only place in that staunchly Muslim country where female staff could wear bikinis.

Nearly every night was party night, and with the Cold War in full swing (Somalia having thrown out the Russians and embraced the 'Land of the Free' for material reasons), we tended to favour Western establishments. Those of the Eastern Bloc remained stiffly aloof from the sometimes raucous goings-on a few paces away. We'd nevertheless wave amicably at each other if we caught an eye but there was hardly any social interplay between the sexes.

I made the Italian Club my base, a flimsy shack with a grass and corrugated-iron roof and enough big fans to make life bearable. No air conditioning, of course, since doors and windows were permanently open. Whatever breeze there was came from the sea, though it could be stifling in the dry season, which lasted eight months of the year, sometimes longer, and was why so many Somalis starved.

The real thrash would begin a little before midnight, when first Franco – and later Gino – both local boys of Italian parents whose families had settled in Somalia between the wars, looked for volunteers for the regular cheetah shoot. I called it a slaughter and they didn't like it, even though the hunts were totally indiscriminate, using big-bore rifles. It was of such frequency while I was there, I was astonished that there were any of these big cats left along this stretch of the coast.

I'd enjoyed good hunting in Africa in my day, and I might have been tempted, but they were running these beautiful animals down in four-wheel-drive vehicles with floodlights, like an Australian kangaroo romp.

Italian Agusta A129 multirole helicopter on the outskirts of the city. (Photo Al. J. Venter)

Towards midnight, the Somali 'ladies' would appear out of the dark. These girls were tall and unassuming, most reflecting an air of diffidence, almost as if the world belonged to them which, I suppose, it did. More salient, as the posters would say, they were strikingly beautiful. They were also incredibly slender in their *kikoi* skirts, usually with nothing on underneath. Some seemed to be blessed with the grace of a desert gazelle.

It did not take any of us hacks very long to appreciate that, in the main, young Somali women are blessed with high cheek-bones and beautiful soft eyes.

Eventually, it was internecine strife that put a stop to all that fun. The generals who took over the country, after they murdered President Abdirashid Ali Shermarke, were soon squabbling among themselves. Then the real killings began, followed by the creation of an artificial nationalism that defied description.

For reasons best known to himself, President Siad Barre dubbed it 'scientific socialism', whatever that was supposed to suggest. As a consequence, government functionaries who had ensconced themselves in Mogadishu's long-defunct parliament laid claim to a lot of territory that was not theirs: it belonged to their neighbours. Barre vigorously said that huge stretches of Ethiopia belonged to Somalia. Essentially, he wanted it all back.

Barre blundered badly when he sent his army into Ethiopia's Ogaden in a bid to enforce that claim. It was Soviet hardware and training that drove them out of that useless strip of desert where nobody lived anyway.

Thereafter, the Somalis demanded the former French colony of Djibouti, but the Elysées Palace warned in stringent terms that if they wanted to go to war about that claim as well, then the French army and air force would be happy to oblige because they needed target practice. That terse off-the-record warning immediately ended the claim and we heard no more about it. But it was also the start of the kind of discord that wracked this nation for almost half a century. Subterfuge, insurrections, intrigue by the bucketful, and army mutinies have continued ever since.

More recently, al-Qaeda got into the act. Mark Bowden gave us a pretty good insight into that mayhem in his classic *Black Hawk Down*. It is about as accurate and brilliant a depiction of any I've seen before or after the American attempt at trying to bring sense to a nation that doesn't understand the word.

There were other, less dramatic aberrations, but the final crunch for the people of Mogadishu came when some government functionary was paid a bribe to allow a local businessman to build a slaughterhouse just outside the town and dump camel guts into the lagoon. Soon all the sharks in the Indian Ocean were assembled off the Somali coast and attacks on humans became so frequent, that every single foreign embassy forbade its staff and nationals to swim in the waters off Mogadishu.

I went back to Somalia early in 1993, not long after the first American soldiers landed on Mogadishu beach with a spectacular show of amphibious force, their faces blackened, flak-jackets in place and M16s at the high port. They were astonished to be greeted by dozens of television crews who had been watching the pantomime from the shore.

It was planned as an invasion and it probably was, though it ended in farce. While some officers were expecting trouble, there was none, staying that way until a bunch of GIs started banging Somali heads together as soon as they fanned out across the airport.

The trouble was, the few Somalis they encountered – the rest of the population was hiding in their homes – happened to be legitimate. Almost all of those at the airport were working with United Nations units already in the country. A few sharp words were exchanged between the UN commander and the American officer in charge before these Rambo wannabees were curtailed.

American participation in Somalia, Operation Restore Hope was hardly a war. There were twenty-two nations involved, as diverse as France, Turkey, Egypt, Italy, Oman, Saudi Arabia, Zimbabwe, Pakistan and Botswana. Few of the soldiers had ever heard a shot fired in anger, much less fought in a war.

Saudi Arabian Humvee.
(Photo Andrew
W. McGalliard)

49

Thirty-thousand strong, they faced a mixed bag of Somali warlords, including a rather crafty rogue and former US Marine by the name of Mohamed Farah Aideed, who had done much to bring the country to its knees. For years, he had purloined food intended to feed the country's starving millions, exporting much of it to neighbouring states for profit.

Meanwhile, all these tribal *padroni* had acquired a formidable arsenal of modern weapons from just about every country on earth. These included British landmines from the Second World War, mostly taken out of the Libyan Desert, Russian small arms, landmines and rocket-propelled grenades, Italian, Spanish, Brazilian, Chinese, Portuguese and American rifles, as well as a miscellany of heavier weapons from South Africa, Germany, Iran, Syria, North Korea, France and elsewhere. If it could kill, or cripple, the ferocious rabble in the streets of Mogadishu got their hands on it.

The truth is, foreign troops in Somalia were on more of a 'rescue mission' than as any kind of fighting force. They had lost sight of the plight of a million or so starving children that had brought them all together in the first place. As soon as things turned nasty, most of the countries that had deployed their soldiers there couldn't wait to get them out. They argued along the lines that the Somalis could settle their own differences – it was their pigeon anyway and, I suppose, they were right.

As it happened, the Americans led the retreat. Despite the loss of life that Mark Bowden wrote about –the entire deployment was actually quite a commendable event – Washington's effort amounted to little more than a brief footnote in history.

Remarkably, my own visit was not prompted by any wish to experience another war, or to join the hordes of journalists already packed into the few hotels that were still open for business. I had recently almost finished my latest book *The Chopper Boys*, and I wanted something unusual to take it into the 1990s.[1] What better place than a troubled corner of Africa where there were a hundred modern and well-equipped American helicopters responsible for most of the communications, supplies and air-combat roles in which the UN had become engaged?

First impressions after landing at Mogadishu Airport on that assignment were instructive. I hadn't expected to find dozens of wrecked aircraft lying at the far end of the runway – Chinese and Soviet MiGs, Sukhois, a few British-built Canberra bombers and American C-47s. The place was an aviation junkyard. Curiously, had somebody put their mind to it, most of those machines might have been salvageable. I'd seen some of those wrecks on previous visits, but they had since been joined by scores more.

The airport was in total disarray, looking as if it had been repeatedly bombarded and nobody had bothered to repair the damage. In fact, things were being fixed, but each time more mortars or RPG-7 rockets would come screaming in.

I recall that the words 'Welcome to Mogadishu Airport' were still legible, with a few of the letters missing, on the main terminal building, part of whose roof was missing. I also recall reporting at the time that not a single pane of glass in the building was intact.

When we emerged from the USAF Hercules that had brought us from Mombasa, we were met by an Arab soldier, who didn't even bother to check our papers before herding us into a rattletrap bus that had once belonged to the Mogadishu municipality. We might have been anyone.

It took me several hours to cadge a lift to the United Nations Operation in Somalia, UNOSOM, headquarters north-east of the airport, where, I reckoned, I'd be able to put phase two of my plan into effect. The force guarding the airport was about to be relieved, I was told. That meant that I could join one of the convoys heading into the city, and from there to the UN compound.

'But first, you must sign this indemnity, if you please,' an Egyptian officer said. 'If you get killed or wounded, there can be no claim on the United Nations.'

I signed. What else was there to do?

Since we'd all be travelling through hostile territory on the back of a truck, the pre-convoy briefing was specific:

'Keep to the middle of the vehicle and stay well down. Don't expose yourself ... they snipe at us from time to time. If we stop and they climb on board, hold on to your bags, your wallet, your spectacles and anything else of value. If you don't, they'll steal everything that isn't bolted down.'

The instructions came from a rather cynical Canadian soldier who had clearly had enough.

With that we were off into Mogadishu proper, or what American 'grunts' like to refer to in their letters home as 'The Dish'. A column of five UN vehicles, escorted front and rear by French armoured personnel carriers (APCs) with their hatches shut, was our escort group. I took up a position behind a group of Gulf soldiers manning a .50 Browning, while the rest of our 'protectors' sat with their weapons cocked, facing outwards. We drove past the old Russian compound, then turned left before reaching the Villaggio Quattro Chilometri.

The backbone of US forces was its crack 10th Mountain Division, based at the airport, Baledogle. (Photo Al J. Venter)

Suddenly I was in a world stranger than anything I had ever known before, even second hand. Nor was it for lack of experience. I had been in Beirut when the Israelis invaded Lebanon in 1982 and that had some sort of shape to it. It was dangerous, sure, but under control, and as they said at the time, 'ordered chaos'. Mogadishu, in contrast, was pandemonium.

Simply put, the city, then and now, sprawls. Approach it from the sea during the monsoon and it's an awesome mish-mash of muddy pools, piles of garbage, open sewers and, everywhere, the turmoil of acres of pullulating crowds. The conglomeration stretched as far as you could see, and in sheer size, the numbers were extremely intimidating.

Just about every building we passed had been blasted. The road from the airport into the city was lined with the wrecks of cars, trucks and armoured personnel carriers, the majority blown apart in countles battles for control. A burnt-out Humvee, already chequered erratically by streaks of rust, spoke of events of months before. There was a time when any American military possession was fair game for Aideed's ragtag horde.

As everyone was only to discover afterwards, there was no clear line of demarcation between the radical factions that opposed our presence. Every man on Mogadishu's streets, as well as the streets of every other town and village in the country, carried a weapon, which often included youngsters not yet 10 years old. Women, children, the old, the crippled and the maimed milled about in and out of who knows how many narrow alleys. There were hundreds of paths and improvised weapon-pits between the few structures that still stood intact.

The road itself was impassable in parts. Jagged blocks of concrete, oil drums and wrecked cars had been hauled across the pot-holed tarmac, obviously intended to slow down the movement of traffic. Pools of filthy green water from the monsoons stagnated in every open patch, in which children were playing.

When we reached the marketplace, having come into view shortly after we'd passed 27th October Square, the throng overflowed farther onto the road and the convoy slowed to a crawl. The entire route had become a souk.

Food and military supplies being unloaded in Mogadishu harbour. (Photo Al J. Venter)

People were shouting, gesticulating at us, at each other, arms flailing, faces contorted. The eyes of some were glazed, others bloodshot, clearly the effects of qat, the amphetamine leaf that everybody on the Horn chews.

One of the soldiers on board told me that near this same market, American Blackhawks had been hit by RPGs, twice in the past few weeks. One of the aviators had been killed and those who'd survived were mauled.

He pointed at a mass of twisted metal lying just off the road, steaming from a squall that had just passed through.

'That was a helicopter,' he declared.

It might well have been since it was unrecognizable. It took a little longer, but we eventually drew into the American diplomatic compound with its heavy-weapon bunkers bristling with large-calibre guns.

'We leave you here,' said the soldier. 'You go now,' he pointed his carbine towards some buildings and smiled when I thanked him in Arabic, '*Shukran.*'

The big UN flag on its pole on the roof of the tallest building hardly stirred, but it did tell me that I'd reached the headquarters of the American commander of UNOSOM, the United Nations operations in Somalia.

I didn't stay long in Mogadishu. Following an identity check, I was sent to the office of Lieutenant Colonel Fred Peck, a Marine officer whose job it was to deal with the foreign correspondent community in what had become a very dubious enterprise for the Americans.

Empty US Army coffins stacked at Mogadishu Airport. (Photo Al J. Venter)

US Air Force Lockheed C-130 Hercules heading to Mogadishu from Mombasa. (Photo Al J. Venter)

Very much as in the summer of 2007, another American officer told me years later, the US Congress was baying for 'our boys' to get the hell out of that African shit hole. Placating journalists every day, Colonel Pack simply couldn't afford to put a foot wrong.

A charming, forthright veteran of several American military ventures of his own, including Vietnam, this professional soldier had been there and, over the years, had done all that it entailed.

What he didn't do was stand on ceremony. The first time I approached him and told him about the book and why I had come to Somalia, he looked me over carefully for a few seconds before I added that I wasn't much interested in East Africa's starving millions. Instead, I explained what I wanted and showed him the printer's dummy of *The Chopper Boys* drawn up for the Frankfurt Book Fair.

'Yep,' said Peck. 'Reckon you really do have a different sort of need.' He addressed one of his officers standing nearby. 'Take Mr Venter here to Marty [Major Martin Culp II] and let's see whether we can get him up to Baledogle in a day or two. They can fly him out on one of the Hawks,' he ordered.

4. SOMALI AFTERBURN

The Battle of Mogadishu, also referred to as the 'Battle of the Black Sea', or for Somalis '*Ma-Alinti Rangers*', 'The Day of the Rangers', was a battle that was part of Operation Gothic Serpent, fought in Mogadishu in early October 1993. Forces of the United States, supported by UNOSOM II, fought against Somali militia fighters loyal to warlord Mohamed Farrah Aidid.

For all that was happening just then in Mogadishu, as Third World or, more pertinently, African conflicts go, there were a number of significant firsts for this so-called Somali peacekeeping force. For a start, there was no 'peace' to maintain. Belligerent factions were battling each other throughout and they continue to do so.

Women played a major role. Females, often under constant threat in an Islamic community, served in many military capacities. These included being pilots of helicopters, gunships and medical evacuation (medevac) aircraft, Australian military police and convoy escorts, members of British air and ground crews, Scandinavian and Canadian flight engineers, medical personnel, drivers, general duty soldiers and guards. In American uniform they performed all these duties and more.

This was also the first conflict in which both aid personnel and the media had taken the first tentative steps either to demonstrably arm themselves or, at the very least, in order to simply stay alive, to acquire weapons for guards hired for their protection.

Professional media personnel in places like Vietnam, Rhodesia, Lebanon and elsewhere would very occasionally arm themselves, but that was a matter of personal choice, and certainly not commonplace. I carried a .45 ACP (automatic colt pistol) in the Rhodesian war and thought nothing of it. In some of the attacks against insurgent or government positions in Angola, I was armed, as I was when I went into combat with some of the mercenary groups that I accompanied over the years, Sierra Leone and El Salvador included.

But that was a matter of choice, and one not always appreciated by some of one's colleagues. In Africa, I'd always argue, you did not wave your press card over your head when you had a hyped-up on who-knows-what murderous thug

US Army pilot at the controls of his Black Hawk. (Photo Al J. Venter)

coming at you with an AK. In Somalia, it was the accepted norm that firearms decided the day. Those with them, survived: those without, well, there were a few.

It was out on the open road that both civilians and the military were at their most vulnerable. In places, Somalia had regressed from a reasonably organized community once ruled by the Italians, into an obscure medieval fiefdom where only might was right.

It was the single example that underscored the age-old premise of even the worst kind of government is better than no government at all. That's the way it was – no control, no order and no law enforcement. There was almost nothing of anything that was needed by this most basic society, with the result that schools, clinics, law courts, or even something as basic as traffic control, were said to exist, but only on paper.

Ostensibly, a United Nations presence was there to cope with this catastrophe, which is what it had devolved into, arguably the biggest humanitarian disaster since the Second World War. More salient, it was a community that appeared to thrive on chaos. Even Cambodia's Pol Pot regime, violent as it was, had fundamental systems of control in place. Also, to a lesser extent, does the Congo. The Somali people, in contrast, existed in a self-made limbo that was little more than a vacuum.

Give the UN its dues, it did try to bring a modicum of order to an extremely confused situation and lost a lot of lives in the process.

Examining individual logbooks along the road between Mogadishu and Baledogle, the only route where I ventured out into the open, with a heavy escort in tow, I discovered that every UN roadblock showed evidence of weapons in international aid vehicles. In each case, the mostly expatriate personnel were identified, serial numbers of the firearms listed, and the weapons then handed back to their owners for the rest of the journey. Significantly, this had never happened with aid personnel in places like Ethiopia, or even Namibia before it became an independent state.

In contrast, weapons found among Somali citizens were confiscated – no argument – but there seemed to be an endless supply of them. By early 1994, it became clear that, in spite of efforts to counter this inflow, more weapons' shipments were reaching the warlords each month, a large proportion of them from the Yemen, ferried across the Red Sea by small, high-powered boats. This begs the question, who was paying for this largesse? Quite a lot of it, we discovered afterwards, came from Iran, the rest from the former Soviet Union and its former Eastern Bloc allies.

My old friend and colleague, the late Mohamed 'Mo' Amin, who at that stage was managing the Reuters Television and News Service in Somalia from Nairobi, admitted that he had acquired four AK-47s at $100 each for the protection of his crews. He declared firmly that his journalists were not armed, only their guards. These weapons did not prevent three members of a Visnews team, including Dan Eldon, from being hacked to death by Somali militiamen in mid-1993. Three months later, five CNN drivers were slaughtered by a militia band. They had been armed and the incident occurred in the presence of hundreds of people as it took place in daylight.

Other journalists, though reluctant to be drawn on the matter, were known to have been carrying weapons, but they would skirt the issue when asked. Not to carry a weapon for self-defence in the streets of Mogadishu, or Kismayo in the early days of the UN presence, could lead to serious consequences, such as getting murdered, one of them explained.

While this writer was in Mogadishu, a French journalist, who approached the US Military Headquarters compound next door to the American Embassy, was accosted by a Somali with a pistol. Without warning, the gunman shot the Frenchman in the arm, which was surprising as it all happened within metres of the US Marine guard post. The journalist fell to the ground, and moments later the American soldier on duty killed the Somali with a burst of automatic fire.

A final word on Mohamed Amin. It was one of the supreme ironies of Mo's life that he died at the hands of a bunch of crazy Islamists who had indirect ties to Somalia. At the time, he was on board an Ethiopian Airlines passenger jet that had been hijacked after taking off from Addis Ababa and ordered to fly to the Indian Ocean Comoros archipelago, even though there was insufficient fuel. The plane crashed in shallow waters, directly opposite a Comorian tourist beach. Mo was one of 117 of the 163 people on board who perished. Typically, the always stroppy Mo wrestled with his attackers before the plane went down, which tells you a lot because he had only one

American Bell Model 209 AH-1 Huey Cobra gunship, Operation Restore Hope, Somalia. (Photo Al J. Venter)

arm. He had lost the other when an ammunition dump exploded a few years before in the Ethiopian capital.

As a relief operation, the Somali campaign was, as one wag phrased it, 'an unmitigated calamity'. By May 1993, when the main body of the American force had left, conditions deteriorated even further. Observers who are familiar with the country pointed to several problems that were never really dealt with properly.

The first and most significant issue was the inability of the UN, or anyone else, to limit the clout of the Somali faction leaders. One very well-known foreign correspondent who was 'in-country' while I was there, said that the only way to bring peace to Somalia would be to put all the warlords against a wall and shoot them. Either that, or pull all United Nations personnel out of the country immediately, he added. Harsh words.

It has been admitted by every single spokesman or officer who had been in the country for any length of time, that there was simply no effective alternative but to remove the warlords from power, unless it was accepted that Somalia would be in a permanent state of anarchistic turmoil. That, however, also ignores the basic premise that they needed to catch these individuals first. The one effort made in this direction by Washington led to the infamous 'Black Hawk Down' disaster.

Most civilian and military personnel who I spoke to in Mogadishu regarded these tribal leaders as primitive and brutal, heedless of the suffering and deaths of the innocent. Most, it soon became apparent, were bent on acquiring more weapons, plenty of qat to which they are addicted and more 'real estate' belonging to other tribes.

A look at the records of some of these adversaries – such as those that are anywhere near complete – is instructive.

The best-known and more obstreperous of the warlords was Mohamed Farah Aideed who, before he died in a fire-fight in Mogadishu in mid-1996, was a seasoned military tactician. At the same time, as the UN quickly discovered, he was devious, unreliable and not averse to confrontation. Aideed's father drove the former dictator Said Barre out of Somalia and 'ruled' over parts of southern Somalia as well as Mogadishu's southern sector for years before the UN arrived.

North Mogadishu was almost totally in the hands of Ali Mahdi Mohamed, a former hotelier who, like Aideed, was also addicted to qat. That was not

Helicopter patrol, Somali coast, with a plane wreck on the beach. (Photo Al J. Venter)

unusual; almost every adult Somali chews the leaf. It is, nevertheless, catego-
rized by UN agencies as a drug.

Colonel Mohamed Said Hersi Morgan, who called himself General Morgan,
had been closely linked to the former president, Barre, his father-in-law.
Morgan's people were dominant in Bardera and parts of the region round the
port of Kismayo, several hundred kilometres south of Mogadishu.

Morgan's principal adversary, for a while, was Colonel Omar Jess, the man
who dominated most of Kismayo. Jess waged war against almost every one
of the fourteen warlords, but just then he was allied to General Aideed, at
least until he was murdered and replaced by another tyrant. At the time, the
Americans were aware that Aideed and Jess proposed to split the country
between them: Aideed the north, and Jess in control of the south.

Few of these self-appointed leaders, megalomaniacs almost to a man, had any
real military or political experience, but they had the hardware, and they were
ruthless. Until the Americans and some of the other coalition forces began to
use force to separate the hordes, or at least to deprive them of their arsenals,

they tended to regard all foreigners with contempt, a trait, history has shown, that is found in some primitive societies. Also, they displayed this animosity with enthusiasm. If they believed they could get away with it, they would fire at every UN patrol that came within range, often using women and children as shields. When the UN retaliated, they would shout foul.

In the early days, with the arrival of the Americans, things changed for the better, and within a comparatively short space of time. Within the first two months, there were more than a dozen air and ground attacks, mostly led by US, Belgian and French forces on known warlord strongpoints all over the country. Some were successful and huge quantities of weapons were seized.

Elsewhere, they failed dismally, mainly because the Americans had a self-defeating habit of dropping leaflets on the towns that they intended to attack in an attempt to warn innocent people to keep clear. That, of course, gave the clan leaders time to stow their goods.

The French, with generations of experience in African conflicts, weren't prone to protocol and invariably went straight in. If there were civilians in the way, it was considered bad luck, but it is instructive that of all the forces deployed in Somalia during this critical period, Paris took among the lowest casualties. The warlords knew better than to goad France.

While the stoning of coalition forces and the occasional sniping attack continued unabated in some parts, mostly where the US forces were active, as initially they were not allowed to use live ammunition to retaliate, such acts stopped where French, French Foreign Legion, Turkish, Australian and some other national troops dominated.

Looking back on the tragedy that was Somalia, it was clear from the start, though hardly ever publicly admitted, that the Americans and the United Nations entered a country deeply in a state of anarchy.

There was no potable water until it was produced by the UN. No electricity, and no effective military or civil administration. The roads everywhere had not been touched since the early 1970s. The capital, Mogadishu, and every other town along the coast and in the interior, showed the results of years of intense and barbarous fighting. To this observer, it seemed like an only slightly less intense version of Beirut at its worst.

Due to the fact that the removal of the dead was well down the list of priorities of any of the warring leaders, the danger of epidemics was real enough for Washington to take extraordinary precautions, which included

US Army patrol briefing prior to setting out from Baledogle air base. (Photo Al J. Venter)

vaccinations for all personnel on a scale that had never before been experienced. We noted in some areas, where bodies had been buried, that the cadavers were hardly covered by the soft sand, and skeletal hands and feet would sometimes appear after a strong wind. Although there were no dogs in Mogadishu – they had all been eaten – jackals, vultures and hyenas dug up many corpses. P.J. O'Rourke, after a visit to Mogadishu at about the same time I was there, had his own take on this situation. He said something along the lines of people not dying like flies in Somalia, because with all those bodies around, the flies were extremely well fed.

There were reports of cholera and other infectious diseases from every aid centre that fielded a responsible presence. There was a huge increase in the incidence of tuberculosis, measles and meningitis among the ill-fed children and adults already trying to cope with kwashiorkor and rickets.

Malaria had been endemic in the whole region since the beginning of time and it was a serious issue when the Americans arrived. In the first months there were many reports coming in of the disease among servicemen, some of them critical enough for relocation to hospitals in Europe. The fact was that almost all anopheline malarial strains along the Indian Ocean coast show strong resistance to available anti-malarial drugs.

As a prophylactic, the medical officer at Baledogle gave me doxycycline hyclate antibiotic tablets, which is more generally used to cure light venereal and amoebic infections. I had some explaining to do when I got home and my wife found the pills in my toiletry bag.

The result of this dislocation was that American and UNOSOM forces were obliged to bring with them every single item that they might need on the deployment. That included food, equipment, medical supplies, fuel, power, spares, machinery and water necessary for the maintenance of tens of thousands of men and women.

Drinking water alone had, very early on, became a factor that needed to be dealt with quickly. Most of it, in plastic bottles, was shipped or, initially, flown in from the Gulf or from Kenya, and sometimes from Europe.

From the start, the European contingents provided their forces with bottles of water from home. The Italians and the French were immovable – they would drink nothing else. They were proved right. Bottled water that came through from Saudi Arabia was found by chemists attached to US forces to be contaminated by faecal matter. Mountains of pallets of water, some 40ft high, most of it stacked near Mogadishu Airport, were destroyed. Millions of dollars were lost because so much of it had come by air.

The Americans took alternative steps. Accompanying their force was a ship specially built for desalinating seawater. It took a little while but the engineers on board eventually made a connection to a shore station with a flexible hose. Within a month they had established two more desalination plants on shore, each capable of producing half a million litres of fresh drinking water a day. Even so, it was rationed.

Up-country, in places like Baledogle, Bardera, or Kismayo on the coast to the south, the problems were not so simple. Some local water sources were purified for washing and bathing, but all drinking water, almost for the duration, was still ferried in by road or air.

During my time at Baledogle in the interior, I counted several C-130s landing or taking off each day, many of them hauling in loads of drinking water on pallets.

If at the time that the United Nations withdrew its forces from Somalia in the early 1990s there was anybody who believed that this chronically afflicted,

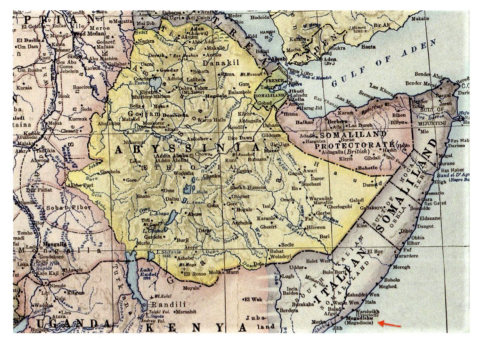

The Horn of Africa, 1922. (Map National Geographic)

Somali National Army (SNA), Independence Day, 1 July 2015. (Omar Abdisalan)

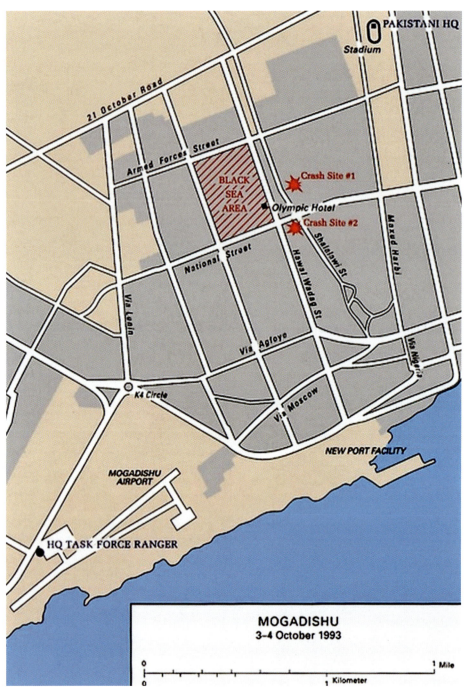

Battle of Mogadishu showing the crash sites of the two American Black Hawk helicopters. (Map US Army)

Above: Former mercenary Arthur Walker (right) who preceded Neal Ellis as Puntland's lone helicopter pilot. (Photo Roelf van Heerden)

Below: Aérospatiale SA-330 Puma, during a vertical replenishment from the USS *Anzio*, Combined Task Force 151, on anti-piracy operations off the Somali coast. (Photo Mathew J. Diendorf)

USMC dress, Middle East, 1991. (Image Donna J. Neary)

General Joseph P. Hoar, USMC, Commander-in-Chief US Central Command, presents a plaque to a Pakistan general, commander of UN ground troops in Mogadishu. (Photo US Department of Defense)

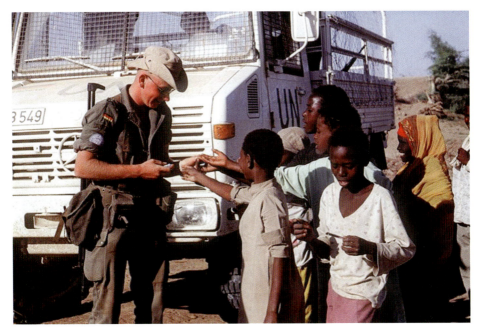

A German soldier with UN forces hands out sweets to children, Operation Continue Hope, Somalia, 1993. (Photo G.D. Robinson)

Belgian troops with UN forces on parade, Operation Continue Hope, Somalia, 1993. (Photo G.D. Robinson)

AMISOM Kenyan troops en route to liberate Kismayo from al-Shabaab, October 2012. (Photo Stuart Price)

AMISOM Ugandan soldier pauses as a tank drives past into al-Shabaab-held northern extremes of Mogadishu, January 2012. (Photo Stuart Price)

Russian-made ZU-23 on display at the 54th anniversary of the SNA celebrations held at Defence Headquarters, 12 April 2014. (Photo David Mutua)

A pick-up truck carrying SNA soldiers in the central Somali town of Belet Weyne, November 2012. (Photo Stuart Price)

SNA soldiers on an operation to capture the Afgoye Corridor, May 2012. (Stuart Price)

President Hassan Sheikh Mohamud (in white cap) during the SNA 55th anniversary celebrations, Defence Headquarters, 12 April 2015. (Photo Omar Abdisalam)

MiG-21 graveyard at Mogadishu Airport. (Photo Al J. Venter)

dyspeptic nation, in the final throes of a self-induced death rattle could ever be a threat to anyone, they were right. In fact, once the Americans moved out, Osama bin Laden's al-Qaeda cohorts quietly shuffled in and established a series of powerful jihadist cells in Mogadishu.

In some respects, conditions in this vast country, that covers an area of a quarter of a million square miles – fractionally smaller than the state of Texas – began to resemble Afghanistan at a time when the Taliban still strode tall in that mountainous kingdom. Once American and European intelligence agencies started to focus on what was going on in the Horn of Africa, it was discovered that Somalia's revolution, like a miasmic virus, had infected an entire region, all the way south, through Kenya and Tanzania to Mozambique and beyond.

More immediate evidence of this development came when a bunch of Mogadishu-based revolutionaries blew up the American embassies in Nairobi and Dar es Salaam in 1998. In the Kenyan capital, more than 200 people were killed and 4,000 injured. Damage caused in Dar es Salaam was not nearly as severe, as the bomber apparently detonated his device prematurely.

That was followed in November 2002 by another group of Islamist dissidents trying to destroy an Israeli-owned Boeing 757 passenger jet with 261 passengers and ten crew on board at Mombasa, Kenya's largest port. Incompetence caused both rockets to miss the plane, but a suicide bomber did ram a truck loaded with explosives into one of that city's Israeli-owned seaside complexes, killing a dozen tourists and staff.

Gradually, there were issues linked to Somalia that began to unravel. For instance, a US Embassy official in Nairobi described it as a situation in which al-Qaeda members were moving into other East African countries like Kenya and Tanzania, where they either used money to buy the allegiance of poor Muslims, or passed themselves off as simple men looking for a quiet place to lead a devout life.

'These people put large amounts of money on the table, and sometimes marry local girls with the idea of establishing a bloodline. In this way, they have managed to forge a formidable network throughout Eastern Africa,' the American declared.

What also emerged were the identities of the people who were involved, almost all of them with Somali connections. For years, Fazul Abdullah Mohammed, mastermind of two Kenya bombings, together with his co-conspirator Saleh Ali Saleh Nabhan, sought out like-minded compatriots in the thousands of mosques that dot this remote coastline. Fazul, a Comorian national, even financed a soccer team in the village of his choice and, in a brash moment, called it the al-Qaeda team.

By all accounts, says a report from the UN, published by All Africa Global Media, Fazul remained in hiding in the Somali capital for years, though he slipped back into Mombasa for a short while, prompting terror alerts from Britain and the US. Like some of his co-conspirators, Fazul survived on cash allowances provided by an al-Qaeda financial controller living in the Sudan.

Following the uncovering of caches of al-Qaeda documents in Afghanistan, several Somali sites, including bases at Las Anod in the north and El Wak near the Kenyan and Ethiopian frontiers, have been pinpointed as two of the most important al-Qaeda training bases in Africa.

It was common knowledge in Nairobi that another al-Qaeda staging post was situated south of the port of Kismayo, not far from the Kenyan border.

Night operations. Burundian troops with the African Union Mission in Somalia.
(Photo AMISOM Public Information)

This was the same facility that was originally implicated in the terrorist bombing of US embassies in Nairobi and Dar es Salaam; explosives used in both attacks came from that specific camp before they were sent by road to Kenya and Tanzania. Each time, we have been told in evidence, there were Somali couriers in charge.

More worrying, some of those involved in a suicide bomb attack on the USS *Cole* in Aden harbour had Mogadishu connections. A Somali woman, identified as paymaster, had acquired the vehicles needed for the operation.

An important consequence of these developments is that American defence planners are considering several sites in Somalia for expanding a military presence in the region.

Several small groups of American special forces are known to have used Ethiopian military bases to stage reconnaissance missions into the interior of Somalia. Following the CIA meeting with Ethiopian President Meles Zenawi, they clandestinely met with several northern dissident tribal leaders Among these dissidents were the commanders of the Rahanweyn Resistance Army (RRA).

Somalia is not the only al-Qaeda casualty. In January 2004, a US State Department advisory cautioned against a resurgence of terrorism in Djibouti, despite – or possibly because of – the presence of large numbers of American and French military personnel. The consular information sheet makes the point that there was an increase in Somali- and Yemeni-inspired terrorism in Djibouti itself, as well as in all its neighbours, and that conditions 'present the potential for internal unrest in the tiny Red Sea enclave'.

What has also become apparent more recently, is that, in spite of Western operatives working in just about every country along the Indian Ocean littoral, with the exception of Somalia and the Sudan, the region continues to remain porous to al-Qaeda agents. This, irrespective of the presence of a variety of American, French, German, British and other naval ships and patrol craft operating in offshore waters.

While several al-Qaeda-funded dhows, loaded with drugs and other illegal paraphernalia intended for East African ports, have been interdicted in the Persian Gulf, the official consensus is that these represent a tiny proportion

Routine VBSS operations – visit, board, search and seizure – intercept Arab shipping off the Somali coast. (Photo US Navy)

US Navy Super Stallion Ch-53E with .50-cal. machine guns on patrol (Photo US Navy)

of craft ferrying illegal substances, agents and weapons between Asia and Africa. A late-2003 report by a UN panel of experts, responsible for monitoring the arms embargo imposed on Somalia in 1992, added that even this offshore multinational force was incapable of stopping the movement of large shipments of weapons by sea.

Washington has been active in other directions. Earlier, an American special forces team, operating out of a major counter-insurgency base established in the tiny Djibouti enclave where it worked with an unnamed Mogadishu warlord, was instrumental in hunting down and arresting Suleiman Abdalla Salim Hemed, who has since been charged in the United States with playing a leadership role in the East African embassy bombings.

Reports out of Nairobi have indicated that, despite these disclosures, there have been other successes, including the uncovering late last year of a major al-Qaeda network along the Kenyan coast. Police seized weapons, training manuals and terrorist safe houses.

That was followed by the arrest of dozens of suspects wanted for several al-Qaeda attacks in East Africa, including some who were on the FBI's most-wanted list.

5. BALEDOGLE

It seemed like another 10th Aviation Brigade field exercise. A cavalry scout weapons team lifted into the blue African sky. Crew chiefs of the assault helicopter battalion serviced their UH-60 Black Hawks, staff planning continued without a break in the tactical operations centre while mechanics and cooks carried out their usual tasks.

> Captain Tom McCann, Baledogle, Somalia, early 1993.

Baledogle, I was to discover after my brief meeting with Colonel Peck, was the hub of all American army as well as US Marine helicopter operations in the Horn of Africa.

It lay alongside a remote village a bit more than 100km north of Mogadishu. 'Somalia in the raw,' as one of the chopper pilots phrased it, 'a single road in and out of the place going exactly nowhere and a pretty real prospect of a bandit ambush'. As he declared, for anyone going out into the adjacent bush that had more camels and goats than people, you needed a solid strong-arm element with more than just AKs for protection.

The air base had formerly been used as a staging post by the Soviets before Somalia switched sides halfway through the Cold War. At one stage, they had even considered building a factory there to build a local variant of the MiG-21.

CH-53s on the flight deck (Photo US Navy)

'Everything that happens with choppers in this conflict you'll find there,' a female major told me. The army flew mainly UH-60 Black Hawks, while the US Marines came and went in their CH-53 Sea Stallions as well as Super Cobra AH-1W gunships.

Baledogle had originally been chosen by the Russians because of Somalia's isolation and its prime position at the southern end of the Red Sea, conduit of much of Europe's oil from the Persian Gulf. It was never a clever move as this corner of Africa has always been unkind to man.

In fact, it reminded me a lot of the Sahel. Almost all of it was desert, with very little grass cover. The region was covered throughout with stunted thorn bushes, and here and there, a rare, ill-nourished acacia poking through, the only foliage not yet ravaged by animals

This is a hard place in which to survive, probably one of the most inhospitable I'd encountered in decades of covering the African beat as a newsman.

The town near the base was more of an assemblage of semi-derelict low buildings that seemed to be held together by bits of twine, animal skins and wire. It was typically Somali hardscrabble, surrounded as it was by putrefying heaps of garbage. The place had once boasted a clinic, distinctive with its whitewashed walls, but the doctor had long since gone.

From the air, the base looked impressive, but this was misleading. There were a few barn-like concrete buildings that had been built by the Soviets, but that was long ago. Some looked like barracks, others had clearly been headquarters of one form or another. The control tower was skeletal, its roof

AH-1W Super Cobra.
(Photo Dustin Kelling)

71

held up by a dozen, rusty steel struts. Above flew two flags, one American, the other that of the United Nations.

As with Mogadishu Airport, almost every fitting that had not been bolted down had disappeared. There was no glass in any of the windows, while the doors had long ago been plundered for firewood.

Once the Americans got there, they put up several enormous tent-like sheds along the perimeter of the main runway. In fact, these were the first things we spotted as we came in from the south. Always assiduous on foreign soil, it hadn't taken them long to set up their own hangars and workshops, every one of them portable and flown in from Stateside, to be taken down again when they moved on.

Alongside were hundreds of cargo stacks, some two or three storeys high, enough stores, containers, vehicles, aircraft and spare parts to keep the war going for a year. In between stood the tents and a few improvised buildings that served the men and women working there.

As we circled, the pilot pointed at scores of circular metal objects below: jet engines, dozens of them, neatly laid out in the bush, some half-buried in the sand. 'Russian,' the pilot said. 'Once brand-new MiG-21 engines,' he shouted into the mike.

Original control tower at Baledogle, stripped but still in use. (Photo Al J. Venter)

He explained afterwards that Baledogle was to have an assembly plant for MiG-21 fighters, the first in black Africa. All the gear, hundreds of cases of machinery, and spares and other equipment had been brought up to Baledogle in a succession of truck convoys. It now lay scattered about the bush. Unlike the Americans, the Soviets took very little back home with them when they departed.

'We were ecstatic,' said the Somali interpreter, trying to explain what it was all about. 'We were to have our own factories for those planes. Somalia would be a leader in Africa. We thought at the time that there would be work for everybody and that Somalia would become a power. The Russians told us so and, like fools, we believed them.'

His eyes blazed. Then, he added, 'Some bureaucrat killed the project ... stillborn, even as we were digging the foundations.'

Nobody in Mogadishu knows the whole story, or at least, following my own inquiries, they were not telling.

Yet, my informant ventured, millions had been spent in getting that far.

'Millions of roubles,' he scoffed derisively. 'All wasted. Think of the hospitals we could have built ... schools.'

None of us had even heard of Baledogle until Operation Restore Hope. It was arguably the best-kept Soviet secret in Africa, and I could see why.

Scores of abandoned Soviet aero engines intended for a factory at Baledogle. (Photo Al J. Venter)

The Black Hawk had been late in getting to Mogadishu Airport to pick me up. I had to be taken there in a Humvee, one of a new generation of American military vehicles that subsequently became familiar during Operation Desert Storm.

From Colonel Peck's UNOSOM headquarters, we retraced our previous route back to the airport. This time, there was a Marine sergeant standing in a well at the back of the infantry carrier with a metre-long wooden staff that he used to dissuade hopeful Somalis from clambering on board.

The Canadians, however, court-martialled some of their soldiers for doing so. To some in Ottawa, that retribution was considered excessive after some of the journalists used the word 'torture' in their despatches. In fact, following an inquiry afterwards, it was self-defence, pure and simple,

One of my first impressions about the place was that there were a lot of women at Baledogle, including senior officers. Major Pauline Knapp commanded the 159th Medical Company. She joked about her husband, also in the army, who had stayed behind at the base in Germany, to play golf. It was her air wing that was responsible for most medical evacuations in Somalia. Their very appropriate motto was 'Anywhere, Any Place, Anytime – You Call, We Haul'.

Major Pauline Knapp. (Photo Al J. Venter)

Major Knapp had under her command a score of Black Hawks, as well as dozens of pilots to fly them, though she did a lot of the work herself. With her crews, the helicopter unit covered almost the entire country, except the north-east, where the French operated Super Pumas. Her medical company, she reckoned, was there to bring all casualties – and the dead – to field hospitals 'as quickly as is humanly possible'.

The work kept her and her crew busy. If she and her husband could manage a weekend a month together, they were lucky.

At Baledogle I also met Captain Yvette and her husband Colonel James Kelly, who was the executive officer at the base. They had met some years before at a military base in California, serving together through Operation Just Cause in Panama where Yvette flew combat.

At Baledogle the warrant officers, most of them pilots and the majority veterans of earlier wars, had set up a rudimentary open-air mess a short distance from the rest for their exclusive use. In that remote wilderness, it was sheer luxury, so only a select few strangers were invited.

For all that, just about everyone at Baledogle and Mogadishu was on first-name terms, officers included. Major Martin Culp II, United States Army, was Marty to just about everybody. Yet he was a senior air force officer with a good deal to answer for to those at the top of the pile. A helicopter pilot himself, his job at headquarters was to lead a unit that planned daily strikes against hostile groups in the interior. It entailed flying armed helicopters against Aideed's men and those Somalis who opposed him, the qat-chewing Colonel Morgan and the irascible Ali Mahdi Muhamad.

US Marine Corps CH-53E Sea Stallion helicopters at an air base in Somalia. (Photo Al J. Venter)

I met Colonel Mike Dallas, who commanded the 2nd Brigade Headquarters of the 10th Mountain Division, on my first morning at the base. He was the ultimate soldier's soldier, and it showed in his command. He tolerated no laxity, not when you are that far from home, he affirmed. Dallas was one of the first of the American field commanders to arrive in Somalia. He had been instrumental in initially putting together the expeditionary force while the unit was still at Fort Drum, its home base in upstate New York.

While not given to excessively high expectations of the human species, there were some things that surprised even me while I worked in Somalia. One was the decision by the US Congress to pull out most of their troops halfway through the campaign. And not long afterwards, history repeated itself on the Asian mainland farther to the east.

From an initial deployment of 28,000 service personnel in the Horn of Africa, the Americans were finally left with a token force of 6,000. The support that they got from the UN was both weak and lukewarm. It was inevitable that Somalia should revert to anarchy even before the last GI had been flown out. What is not generally accepted about the American effort in Somalia is that while Washington had limited men on the ground in this vast north-east African state, they actually ran the show, gladly so, with few dividends in prospect.

For a start, they played a vital role in separating the factions. If any of the so-called warlords got uppish, he got hit. UH-60 Black Hawk assault helicopters regularly struck at rebel positions in Afghoi, Jilib, Belet Uen and Marka, with Washington very well aware that the enemy forces they were dealing with were hard men armed with an array of serious weapons. The only response to such people, the first Bush administration unequivocally declared, was strong and sustained military action.

What was not generally accepted is that the bloody battle immortalized by Mark Bowden's remarkable book, *Black Hawk Down*, the one that ended catastrophically with the loss of eighteen American soldiers who were trying to capture one of Somalia's most notorious war lords, was actually an ambush that appears to have been planned a long while ahead.

Suddenly, from nowhere, up popped many hundreds of Soviet-supplied RPG-7s, and though they weren't used with much effect, it was numbers that counted in the end. These weapons had all been smuggled into Somalia in the months before that fateful day by forces hostile to the United States. Looking back, one has to concede that it had the required effect.

Within days, the Pentagon had made its decision. It was time for the troops to come home.

Of course, once the American forces had been reduced, there was no possibility that the UN could control developments even remotely as effectively as before. What resulted was another UN fiasco.

Conflict within this society, in recent years, at a conservative count, has cost about half a million lives. That tally includes countless women and children. Famine too, as a consequence of a dislocated society that emerged from continual warfare, has also taken its toll. Essentially, the problem lay in the excesses of more than a dozen Somali warlords that were mindless and often unconscionably brutal.

These tribal or factional leaders were not circumscribed by any convention, Geneva or otherwise. It was fundamentally internecine warfare, one clan pitted against another, come what may. Anybody in the way was of no consequence, which was why so many aid workers, foreign media personnel, innocent civilians, the young, the old, men and women were killed. Anybody in the firing line when there were things happening didn't rate consideration.

Stealth and subterfuge were the norm for the majority of these mindless killers. In that, the Somali nation seems always to have proved particularly adept.

After a while in the country, it became apparent that the Somali fighting man would never make a regular, disciplined soldier. There are exceptions of course, because quite a few of them are remarkable combatants who give their

US Marines UH-60 Black Hawks. (Photo Nicole Hall)

all, with unusual bravery and single-minded dedication as displayed by some locals attached to foreign entities.

However, the majority of these so-called fighters, in realty little more than gun-toting thugs, are rarely regarded by members of international aid contingents, by the media or by the UNOSOM or AMISOM troops, as particularly imaginative, resolute or resourceful.

It was in this pseudo-war that the combined forces of the United Nations and Washington attempted to restore a measure of peace and regulation in one of Africa's utterly lawless regions.

People often forget why the Horn attracted so much attention in the first place, and continues to do so, which is why you have a NATO naval task permanently stationed off Somalia, even as I write. Somalia not only flanks the busiest sea lanes in the world on the Red Sea, a shipping route that conveys about a third of the world's fuel supplies, but also across the way is oil-rich Saudi Arabia.

Due to the nature of the troubles there, said Farouk Mawlawi, a UN spokesman in Mogadishu in mid-February 1993, 'it is not and will not be a passive peace observer group. Force would be opposed with force.'

Somali soldiers stand guard as President Sheik Sharif visits Balad. (Photo AMISOM Public Information)

A Humvee drives through a park of abandoned Russian-made aircraft, Mogadishu. (Photo Al J. Venter)

The hangar at MCAF Beledogle. (Photo US Marine Corps)

6. MOGADISHU MANHUNTS

Pull up 'Battle for Mogadishu' on Google or any other website that offers background to past events in Somalia and you will get any number of articles about the so-called lost lessons of *Black Hawk Down*.

In many of these articles, the events that took place are authoritatively offered, most of the time in graphic detail. They deal with the units, commanders and vehicles involved, the UH-60 helicopters shot down by the jihadi fighters and, of course, the weapons used. Some commentators deal with enemy tactics as well as losses suffered by American units and in some cases, even their names.

The trouble is that few of those giving us the benefits of their wisdom have ever been anywhere near where it all happened. More to the point, the majority of so-called pundits have never even visited Somalia, nor would they, if offered the opportunity.

Mark Bowden, who wrote his classic book on the subject, *Black Hawk Down*, while still working in newspapers, at least took the trouble to put his feet on the ground in Mogadishu and do the kind of research needed, something at which he proved exceedingly good. We communicated afterwards and I suggested that he might have taken his life in his hands in doing research in Africa's Horn. While he did admit that it was the only way, he declared that it was a calculated risk.

Other 'authorities' are not nearly as meticulous (or brave), although Benjamin Runkle, a former Defense Department and National Security official and the author of *Wanted Dead or Alive: Manhunts from Geronimo to Bin Laden*, is instructive. I quote one of his reports, dated 10 March 2013, originally published in the War on the Rocks website under the title of 'The Lost Lessons of 'Black Hawk Down':

Today marks the 20th anniversary of The Battle of Mogadishu, the American operation in Somalia later immortalized by Mark Bowden's seminal non-fiction book *Black Hawk Down* and dramatized in Ridley Scott's exhilarating but slightly less non-fictional movie of the same name. On October 3, 1993, 160 U.S. Army Rangers and other Special Operations forces launched what was supposed to be a routine raid to capture two lieutenants of Somali war lord Mohammed Farah Aideed. But when two MH-60L helicopters providing

80

An abandoned street in Mogadishu, known as the 'Green Line', January 1993.
(Photo R. Oriez / US Department of Defense)

fire support were shot down, the operation became a desperate search and rescue mission in which US forces were besieged overnight by thousands of heavily armed Somali militiamen. Fourteen hours after the operation's start, there were 18 Americans dead, 84 were wounded and one pilot was missing.

The fact is that this incident in Somalia in which American soldiers and airmen died should never have happened. Runkle continues:

> The incredible valour and drama of Task Force Ranger's ordeal over those two days has, unfortunately, tended to draw attention away from the broader campaign to capture Aideed, whom US and international forces had been hunting since the previous June when Aideed's Somali National Alliance ambushed and mutilated 24 Pakistani peacekeepers. This manhunt was part of a broader operation which – along with the Black Hawk Down battle itself – carries important tactical, operational, and strategic lessons.

I have covered many wars in Africa, the Middle East, Central America and elsewhere. Somalia's war, as has since been proved, was totally different to any other African conflict that took place in the past half century.

Proudly African, the average Somali, if you go back thousands of years, probably inherited more Arab blood from his distant forefathers than African, a bit like the Falasha Ethiopians, some of whom share a Judaic heritage that identifies them as Jews and one of the reasons why there are so many Ethiopians in modern Israel today.

Taken together, all this makes the average Somali insurgent a difficult type to fight, as many Americans and Europeans are now discovering for themselves in terror attacks where there are quite often Somalis involved. In Britain in the past decade, a large percentage of terror attacks involved one or more Somalis somewhere within the makeup of a terror group.

The bottom line in the United Nations-backed Operation Restore Hope campaign in Somalia, that lasted from 5 December 1992 to 4 May 1993, was that just about everybody, the Americans especially, did not know or even vaguely understand the Somali psyche, or how they thought or were motivated or that so many of them were basically extreme fanatics. Indeed, as might have been expected, the commanders of the US force treated these individuals on equal terms, as Americans and most Europeans like to do. As a consequence, most Westerners involved in that disaster were brutally exploited by a bunch of warlords who were a lot sharper than anybody believed possible.

Not so the Turks or the Pakistanis whose forces also served in Somalia while the Americans were there. They tended to draw pretty distinct lines in the sand as to what could or could not take place when their own forces were in any particular area. If a group of Somalis were aggressive towards any Turkish

US troops at a vehicle checkpoint, Somalia, 1992. (Photo Monica's dad)

unit it would come under fire and that was that. It also meant that Turkish units deployed in Somalia had fewer problems with the locals than any other national force. The Pakistani Army eventually also put its foot down, but in retrospect, not firmly enough, which was why twenty-four of their soldiers were massacred while inspecting an illegal Somali weapons cache.

Had anybody looked into what was waiting for them prior to going into UNITAF, the Unified Task Force as it was officially designated, they would have been appalled at the lifestyle of the average Somali. For a start, with a lot of exceptions of course, it was, and still is, left to the women to provide for the family.

It is no different today, nor when American marines stepped off their boats at the start of what was regarded in Washington as a rescue mission. The intention, as the name implied, was to give the nation a kick-start to get it back on track again. The question remains: on track for what?

Rome under Mussolini believed in discipline and it obviously had an effect, as, decades after the Italian Army had been kicked out of East Africa, the entire region remained very well ordered. It stayed like that even after Allied forces had moved on and the country gained its independence.

The tyrant Siad Barre, and those before him, also ruled with a heavy hand, which was evident when I visited Mogadishu several times in the late 1960s and 1970s.

There was a good measure of industry, shops were open, open-air vendors were a pleasure to do business with because their wares were all fresh and the people traded with their neighbours. Farther afield, Somali fishing boats roamed across the Indian Ocean. The country's civil service had its place, as did the police and the army. Essentially, Somalia was a place where things worked.

But once law and ordered surrendered to anarchy, everything changed, though not yet to the extent you see in the country today as the Islamic fundamentalist issue had not yet become part of the equation. That said, there were others who were intent on making it so when several Arab states, as well as Iran, started sending in their agents. A new kind of totalitarian civil war emerged with local warlords pitching for favours in order to score points.

Payback on the part of the newcomers was to supply the recalcitrants with weapons and ammunition, all basic stuff and as much as the warlords wanted. For Mohammed Farah Aideed and his gang of ruffians, the weapon of choice was the ubiquitous RPG-7 rocket-propelled grenade.

That all happened not long before Operation Restore Hope was launched. Although Washington was not yet aware of it, thousands of RPG grenades and launchers, together with large supplies of explosives to start making IEDs (something Somali jihadi volunteers had been taught in Central Asia), had begun to clandestinely enter the country from friendly sources in the Yemen and Iran.

At the same time, one needs to understand that the people in this remote region, fringing the southern end of the Red Sea, fought their wars very differently to how we go about things in the West. This corner of north-east Africa remains one of the most primitive regions in the world where, often, fighting to the death is a basic way of life.

Yet, for all that, the conflict was barely covered by the media and even today most people have difficulty recalling the events that had happened, or that a series of regional famines before and after that conflict, in Ethiopia, Somalia and Eritrea, claimed more than a million lives several times in the past fifty years.

Where the Americans made some of their biggest mistakes, according to John Hirsh, a senior adviser at the International Peace Institute and a former US ambassador to Sierra Leone, was encapsulated in an article he did for IPI Global Observatory, published on 13 October 2013.

Titled 'Twenty Years After Black Hawk Down, What Lessons Have Been Learned?', Hirsh makes the most salient point of all: 'Washington took a conciliatory and cautious approach, underscoring that the Somalis had to decide their own destiny.'

House clearance, US troops in Mogadishu, 1993. (Photo Terry C. Mitchell)

He goes on:

The war lords were assured that UNITAF's role was solely to assist in alleviating the famine crisis. Ambassador Oakley urged Somali leaders to enter into political dialogue to establish a new Somali government.

They succeeded in persuading the war lords to set aside their 'Technicals' and open the roads to the delivery of relief supplies. A Civilian-Military Operations Command (CMOC) was set up as a unique and highly successful initiative whereby UNITAF forces accompanied delivery of relief and medical supplies by humanitarian agencies to the afflicted regions in the South. The humanitarian crisis was quickly mitigated if not totally resolved.

Of course, the warlords could not believe their luck, that the Americans, in an initiative led by Bill Clinton, should be so naïve as to actually trust them.

Naturally, the drama surrounding Black Hawk Down had significant ramifications for the Clinton administration's Africa policy, including the decision six months later not to become engaged in preventing the genocide in Rwanda. In that tiny country, about as big as Maryland, between April and June 1994, an estimated 800,000 Rwandans were slaughtered in the space of 100 days, most of them Tutsis.

Benjamin Runkle offers several 'lessons' in his treatise about American involvement in Somalia. Two of these stand out head and shoulders above the others.

The first is titled 'Lesson One: Technology Does Not Guarantee Success'. As he says, Task Force Ranger enjoyed access to the full range of US intelligence capabilities and assets. The Central Spike signals-intelligence team was pulled off the hunt for Colombian drug lord Pablo Escobar in order to assist the search for Mohammed Farah Aideed.

Theatre and joint task-force imagery assets included:

The navy's tactical airborne reconnaissance pod system slung under low-flying jet aircraft;
A specially modified navy Lockheed P-3 Orion patrol plan;
A single-engine, super-quiet airplane with a real-time downlink to the task force headquarters;

The Pioneer unmanned aerial vehicle with a downlink to the oint Operations Centre (JOC); and

The Night Hawk ground FLIR (Forward-Looking Infrared sensor) system.

Yet, these highly sophisticated technological assets were ultimately ineffective because they could not pick up the lower-level technology used by the Somalis. Aideed communicated with his militia by courier and the use of obsolete walkie-talkies too low-powered to be detected by America's electronic eavesdropping equipment.

In other words, when combined with American forces' post-Desert Storm reliance on high-technology, Somalia's complete and utter technological backwardness was actually an asset to Aideed.

'Lesson Two: In Manhunts, the Decisive Terrain is the Human Terrain' is even more specific as it involves intelligence, the human kind.

I quote: 'Task Force Ranger's commander, Major General William Garrison, believed the key to apprehending Aideed was actionable intelligence provided by human intelligence (HUMINT).'

The original plan had called for the CIA's top Somali informant, a minor warlord loosely affiliated with Aideed, to present the former marine with an elegant hand-carved cane with a homing beacon embedded in the head.

The plan seemed fool proof, until half-colonel Dave McKnight, commander of the 3/75th Ranger Battalion and the task force's intelligence chief, burst into Garrison's headquarters at the Mogadishu airport on their first day and exclaimed, 'Main source shot in the head. He's not dead yet, but we're fucked!' The top Somali CIA informant had apparently been mortally wounded in a game of Russian roulette.

By the time Task Force Ranger arrived in Mogadishu in August 1993, the Intelligence Support Activity, Delta Force's special intelligence cell, and the CIA had completely lost track of Aideed, who had not been seen for a whole month.

The Russian roulette incident was the least of their troubles. Looking at the broader history of strategic manhunts from Geronimo to Osama bin Laden, the clearest dividing line between successful and failed campaigns is the human terrain over which the campaign is conducted.

As Runkle emphatically declares, 'Human terrain determines the ability to obtain actionable intelligence on the target, either from the local population or from within the target's network.'

Simply put, if the targeted individual is perceived as a hero or a 'Robin Hood' type of figure, the protection offered by the local population will thwart almost any number of satellites or elite troops. Somalia's social fabric of interwoven clans, tribes and warlords proved a particularly formidable intelligence-gathering challenge.

Moreover, early US conventional force operations often exacerbated the problem. On 12 July 10th Mountain Division forces attacked a meeting of Habr Gidr clan leaders, operating on the belief that Aideed would be present. Instead, they ended up killing numerous clan elders, mullahs and intellectuals, many of whom had in fact opposed Aideed and had counselled accommodation with UN forces.

As American forces withdrew, an enraged Somali mob beat to death four Western journalists who had arrived at the scene to report on the attack. Any remaining Habr Gidr moderates quickly rallied behind Aideed, the attack causing many non-Habr Gidr to sympathize and even ally with Aideed, further drying up the already sparse HUMINT.

Italian army (*esercito*) CH-47C Chinooks at a military base near Mogadishu. (Photo Al J. Venter)

Coastal helicopter patrol. (Photo Al J. Venter)

One of the final observations made by Runkle was:

There is an important observation that we must not ignore, which is that the Americans were not defeated militarily in Somalia. Effective human and economic losses were not inflicted on them. All that happened was that the Somali battle revealed many of their psychological, political, and perhaps military weaknesses. The Somali experience confirmed the spurious nature of American power and that it has not recovered from the Vietnam complex. It fears getting bogged down in a real war that would reveal its psychological collapse at the level of personnel and leadership. Since Vietnam, America has been seeking easy battles that are completely guaranteed.

7. HIDDEN KILLERS

Landmines are a reality: grim and totally uncompromising.

Right now, more of these devices are being laid by the Taliban in those parts of Afghanistan where coalition forces are most active. The same applies to Africa, especially in places like the Congo and more recently, parts of Somalia.

An interesting weapon, the landmine, as deadly and destructive today as it was when first deployed by the Chinese in the thirteenth century.

Robert Bryce, in an insightful article for *The Atlantic Monthly*'s Foreign Affairs,[1] discussed how nearly a century before, while serving as a British liaison officer to the Arab tribes during the First World War, T. E. Lawrence, of Lawrence of Arabia fame, developed many of the techniques of modern insurgency warfare. Lawrence's fluency in Arabic and a profound understanding of Arab culture helped him invigorate the Arab Revolt of 1916–18, while his savvy military tactics certainly ensured its success against the Turks.

He goes on: 'In his memoir, *Seven Pillars of Wisdom* (1922), Lawrence revealed his most effective tactic. "Mines were the best weapon yet discovered to make the regular working of their trains costly and uncertain for our Turkish enemy." If not for Lawrence's pioneering use of precisely placed explosives, the Arab Revolt might well have failed.'

Russian TM-46
anti-tank mine.
(Photo US Marine Corps)

In Iraq, the insurgents are using similar weapons against coalition forces. Today they are called IEDs, Improvised Explosive Devices, rather than mines and the insurgents are targeting automobiles rather than trains. The effect is just as devastating.

The statistics are sobering. The number of mines being used in Iraq, and the share of casualties for which they are responsible, says Bryce, dwarf anything ever before seen by the American military:

> During World War 2 three percent of US combat deaths were caused by mines or booby traps. In Korea that figure was four percent. By 1967, during the Vietnam War, it was nine percent, and the Pentagon began experimenting with armoured boots. From June to November of 2005, IEDs were responsible for 65 percent of American combat deaths and roughly half of all non-fatal injuries.

He explains that detonation techniques are many. The insurgents use pressure switches, infrared beams, cell phones, garage-door openers, and even garden hoses, which, when run over by a vehicle, send a stream of water into a small bottle, activating a detonator.

Curiously, though the use of mines in not as widespread in Somalia, largely because of the vast distances that need to be covered by insurgents, the damage cause by these devices can be sobering.

A stash of lifted anti-tank mines. (Author's Collection)

The landmine problem in Somalia is roughly similar to that of other parts of southern and eastern Africa, which have seen much political and military unrest. It can best be described as a general problem in the southern sectors of Somalia and a very serious one farther north.

Border areas where large numbers of refugees and displaced persons travel are also suspected regions of heavy mine-laying. Though figures are vague and impossible to verify, it is believed that several hundred thousand mines have been emplaced in Somalia during the last few years of uncertainty. Somalia's unsettled condition further influences the problem, including that of location and booby traps.

Large numbers of refugees from Somalia are reported to be in camps in the surrounding countries such as Ethiopia and Kenya. Additionally, there has been a massive displacement of persons within Somalia. These factors, in conjunction with famine, food distribution, political instability, and struggles for local control have influenced landmine use.

As a result, landmines can be expected on travel routes to prevent movement of refugees to, from, and within, Somalia. That said, large minefields will probably have only been laid around previously contested areas that have been considered important.

An example is the area surrounding the city of Hargeisa. Large patterned minefields, exceeding 100,000 mines, the majority of which anti-personnel,

IED-clearing explosive ordnance disposal (EOD) team. (Photo Andrew Guffey)

have been laid in sections surrounding the city. Extensive booby-trap activity has also been reported from Hargeisa.

In Somalia, as elsewhere in Africa, the international community seems committed to handling the problem, but, for a start, nothing can be done before there is a ceasefire in place.

A US State Department survey titled 'Hidden Killers: The Global Problem with Uncleared Landmines'[2] identified almost seventy countries with landmine problems. It also expressed concern at the slow speed that this work was being accomplished and, more importantly, the variable degree of certainty that an area, once certified as clear, is actually completely free of explosives. This has been a recurring problem in places such as Cambodia, Afghanistan, Angola, South Sudan and elsewhere, including Somalia, and is invariably the consequence of ongoing conflict. Africa, with its inordinate range of problems, is likely to be the focus of much of the world's mine-clearing endeavours in the future.

Another problem likely to be encountered in Somalia once mine-clearing operations begin, is that of booby traps, all of which have to be manually dismantled.

There are a variety of devices encountered by the clearing teams in most African states. Apart from a preponderance of Chinese Type-72s, there are numerous Yugoslavian PROM-1 fragmentation and Czech PP-Mi-Sr bounding anti-personnel mines. Also found are Yugoslavian PMR-2As and PMA-3s, Russian PMNs, East German PPM-2s, the full series of Russian PMDs, and just about every ant-tank mine in the book except South African No. 8s.

PROM-1 bounding anti-personnel mine.
(Photo Tracey L. Hall-Leahy)

8. TERROR AND PIRACY

One of the quirks of fighting an insurgency in Africa is that the government involved will quite often know exactly from where a terrorist group like al-Qaeda is operating. For reasons known only to itself, however, it will ignore both its presence as well as any potential threat factor. To some, the situation is sometimes referred to as a 'head-in-the-sand syndrome', the argument being that by tomorrow the menace might have disappeared.

Former South African Air Force (SAAF) colonel and mercenary, Neall Ellis, served in Somalia's remote north for several years, flying a lone Alouette III helicopter attached to the Puntland Maritime Police Force (PMPF).

Though the helicopter was already decades old, and a veteran of Pretoria's border wars, its role was far more illustrious than the unit itself. The makeshift unit,

Gunhip pilot Neall Ellis (second from right) in front of the ageing Alouette III. (Photo Rudolf van Heerden)

British patrol boats from the frigate HMS *Monmouth* stop and search, Arabian Gulf.
(Photo Ministry of Defence)

comprised solely of soldiers of fortune, all land- or sea-bound, offered no co-pilot, no emergency equipment, no backup if something went wrong on a flight into the interior. Added to this, maintenance throughout was at an absolute minimum.

There were flights when Ellis was tasked to fly out to sea and check on suspect boats. That, he confided, was dodgy, since he was never issued with any rescue gear, plus, communications being suspect, if he did go down over open water, there was no guarantee that a boat would be sent out to search for him. Curiously, the people backing his unit were Gulf-state Arabs, all of whom oil millionaires, so the aberration was culpable.

Nellis, as his friends call him, recorded some of the events as they happened while with the Puntland police.

The Puntland-based al-Qaeda-linked terror group, which Ellis and those South African mercenaries who were there before him were tasked to counter, had, and still has, a number of isolated bases in a range of mountains to the immediate east of the main military airport at Bosaso. This is difficult, mountain country with few access paths, making a surreptitious approach by a military squad all but impossible.

Also, while high ground only tops 2,000m, it was labelled by the Puntland authorities as a no-fly zone, as was the case when the gunship was operational. (The helicopter was eventually grounded because of a lack of spares.) The Puntland, however, is not only home to al-Qaeda, housing as it does other insurgency groups.

Ellis told *Jane's Defence Weekly* that it was an open secret that there was a major al-Qaeda base in the desert barely 10km from Bosaso airport, a small town in the north of the country about 500km east of Djibouti. The consensus among expatriates working there was that it was only a matter of time before the sprawling complex came under attack.[1]

It is worth mentioning that the base commander several times asked for permission to launch a strike, but each time the matter was referred to the president in the Puntland regional capital of Garowe, situated in the desert more than 300km to the south. The answer that came back was emphatic: do nothing!

Prior to Ellis flying for the Puntland government, former SAAF helicopter gunship pilot, the late Arthur Walker had the job. He was also a former mercenary who had served with Executive Outcomes in Angola and Sierra Leone.[2]

Apparently not much has changed since Walker went home as the camp is still there. Indeed, it is now well established in the foothills of Puntland's Golis Mountains that fringe this stretch of the north-west Indian Ocean adjacent to the Red Sea. So much so, that each time aircraft or helicopters attached to the Puntland air wing approach, they are fired on by Islamic militants.

The Golis range is ideally situated for use by insurgents as a secure base for moving weapons, explosives and other military hardware needed by al-Shabaab cadres in their war against the authorities and African Union (AU) forces. It says a lot that virtually all the suicide bombs recently detonated in Mogadishu had their origins in Puntland, from where the materiel was taken southwards by road, a distance of about 1,500km.

How these revolutionaries managed to pass unchallenged through dozens of road blocks en route is not certain. Clearly, a fundamentalist network has a lot to do with it.

A reliable intelligence source from Somalia recently returned to his home base in Pakistan, where, in an extensive debriefing, it was disclosed that the northernmost region of this embattled African land had become a focus of al-Qaeda insurgency, intent on infiltrating parts of northern and eastern Africa. For many of them, Puntland was their first point of entry. Also, the bombs employed towards the end of 2013 in the destruction of Westgate in Narobi, Kenya's largest shopping mall, came from there.

Of note here is the fact that Puntland, about the size of Kansas, makes up about a third of Somalia's geographical area. With a population of about four million, Ellis and his associates were expected to cover an enormous area with a single one-engine helicopter.

Moreover, the country has been a semi-autonomous state for almost two decades, having broken away from the central government in 1998, partly because of tribal differences and the fact that locals regarded Mogadishu as 'ungovernable'.

Unquestionably, Puntland's biggest single problem today is one of identity. The fledgling state has not been recognized by a single country. As expected, the territory's original split from the central Mogadishu government did not go smoothly. Immediately after declaring itself independent, sporadic fighting broke out between Puntland and Somaliland over the ownership of the Sool and Sanaag regions, both claimed by Puntland based on ethnicity.

Violence also accompanied a political power struggle in 2001 between rival claimants to the Puntland leadership. Overall, it was, and still is, in a state of flux, hindered by a pervasive al-Qaeda presence.

Security in the Horn of Africa has deteriorated markedly in recent years. In Djibouti, the focus of American military action against Yemeni- and Somali-based militants linked to al-Qaeda, the Pentagon moved its drone operations from Camp Lemonnier, the former French Foreign Legion headquarters on the Red Sea, to an undisclosed location in the desert interior.

The reasons for moving the United States's prime naval expeditionary base in the region to a more secure location were basic. There had been at least half a dozen crashes of these unmanned aerial vehicles, which, Washington declared, had raised safety concerns, not least because many Djibouti nationals have family connections across the border in the Yemeni target region.

The Red Sea operational base has been a major counter-terrorism centre for the Pentagon for more than a decade. The Americans run daily flights of General Atomics MQ-1 Predator surveillance drones across the narrow stretch of ocean into the Yemen and surrounding areas, which have resulted in a series of air-to-ground strikes against Islamist rebel groups.

Al-Qaeda's influence in this enormous region is powerful, stretching all the way from Yemen, through Somalia to Mogadishu, and farther afield into the former British territories of Kenya and Tanzania.

Jubaland Administration soldiers celebrate after rescuing al-Shabaab hostages in Kismayo. Jubaland, on the southern Somali border with Kenya, like Puntland, is yet another autonomous entity within Somalia. (Photo Ramadan Mohamed)

Somalia's capital lies more than 1,000km by air to the south of Djibouti. For decades, the city has been the focus of terrorist activity by al-Shabaab, the most active al-Qaeda affiliate, responsible for terror attacks in several neighbouring countries including Kenya. The murder of dozens of civilians in a Nairobi supermarket in 2013 was a case in point.

Other attacks included car bomb and IED attacks against Western and African Union interests in the city, and a Kenyan university campus at Garissa in 2015 in which 148 students were killed and 79 wounded. Of greater significance, however, have been the numerous attacks on well-defended African Union military elements in Somalia itself.

An even gloomier picture emerged in a more recent report titled 'Is the Coalition Fighting al-Shabaab Falling Apart?' compiled by Joshua Meservey, Policy Analyst, Africa and the Middle East at the Heritage Foundation (a notable authority who spent years in Africa) and Kelsey Lilley, associate director of the Atlantic Council's Africa Centre in the United States.

The terror group launched three deadly attacks in October 2016: another in a town in Kenya, a mosque in Mogadishu, and on an African Union military base in the country's strategically important Hiran region.

More troublingly, they declared, Ethiopian troops abruptly withdrew the same month from a base in Halgan, also in Hiran, the third town that Ethiopian forces had abandoned, though there were reports that they might have pulled out of almost a dozen by the end of 2016. Their report states that 'Addis Ababa has not confirmed why it left Hiran exposed, but it is likely repositioning its forces to respond to large-scale domestic protests that have rattled the Ethiopian government'. They suggest that:

> The strategic Ethiopian withdrawal is problematic because it adds to the growing strains on the African Union Mission in Somalia (AMISOM), the anti-al-Shabaab military coalition, of which Ethiopia is a member. Moreover, ANISOM is due to start leaving Somalia in late 2018, but the growing pressure on its members suggests that an even earlier exit is possible. AMISOM's other major troop-contributing countries, Burundi, Uganda, and Kenya, are all vulnerable to political upheaval of the sort that appears to have Ethiopia contemplating a drawdown.
>
> This should set off alarm bells from Mogadishu to Washington. AMISOM is the only capable ground force battling al-Shabaab, and it is critical to protecting the highly fragile and reversible military gains made against the group.

An all-out fracturing of the mission would have dire consequences for the fight to defeat al-Shabaab.

It is notable that when preparing for a visit to the Somali capital in 2016, this author was warned not to leave the security of the city's airport complex without a reasonably well-armed military escort.

There have been several serious attacks in Puntland itself, including a massive vehicle-borne IED attack on members of the air wing. Ellis was among them when they were on an end-of-the-month visit to the bank in Bosaso town. They were clearly tracked and targeted by insurgents. There were numerous casualties, including several people killed. By some accounts, the Level-6 Ford-350 armoured vehicle took the brunt of the blast, saving the lives of several PMPF members, Ellis among them.

Interestingly, some of the survivors were later debriefed by four of Puntland's senior security officials. Two of those officials had already survived car bomb attacks. In addition, one of them emerged unscathed from an assassination attempt, while a fourth had his Bosaso house burned down in an al-Qaeda attack.

Reports that circulated afterwards disclosed that the bomber was a 30-year-old man who had recently married a widow. He had apparently been recruited by al-Qaeda.

Since then, a lot more has gone wrong in trying to counter insurgency in the Horn of Africa.

Recent reports confirm that al-Shabaab now has access to 82mm mortars, purportedly out of Pakistan and Iran. Because of long-standing arms sanctions against Puntland, government security forces have nothing to match this weapon so are unable to counter this threat, even though detachments of United States Marines are currently training the country's security forces.

The fact is, insurgent groups in Puntland have achieved a significant foothold, and infiltrations from the Yemen are well planned and coordinated. As this expansive desert land lies adjacent to the Saudi Peninsula, insurgents employ small motorized 'go-for' boats and Arab dhows to cross the narrows. This entire region is now regarded as extremely volatile and dangerous by Western intelligence experts.

While Bosaso town, an untidy urban desert sprawl a short drive from the airport, has not been heavily targeted as yet, nobody working for the PMPF goes

Al-Shabaab fighters disengage and lay down arms, 22 September 2012. (Photo AMISOM Public Information)

there without an escort of at least six soldiers, more if possible because of the potential of being blasted by suicide bombers.

Bosaso remains an isolated outpost. Although served by a twice-weekly Antonov flight from Berbera in quasi-independent Somaliland 500km to the west, it is not a reliable link, even if it is the only access by air into the territory.

What does run like proverbial clockwork is the almost new Bombardier Dash-8 aircraft that touches down at Bosaso at 0800 hours every morning with the region's supply of qat.

At the time that I reported on events in Puntland for *Jane's*, there was some disquiet among those working for Puntland's air wing, in part because the 40-year-old Alouette, with a single mounted PKM machine gun, was simply not up to the task of covering the vast distances required of it.

In an effort to remedy the situation, Ellis – always the pragmatist – suggested that a MBB/Kawasaki BK117 helicopter (a 9-seater in a two-plus-seven configuration), be acquired by the Garowe administration. The antiquated Alouette (potentially one-plus-six) could take only the pilot and two passengers over the long distances that this machine was required to traverse with a full load of fuel.

He explained that from Bosaso, the flying time to Garowe was ninety minutes, then another ninety minutes to Bargaal, followed by an even longer haul to get to the coastal town of Hafun.

In between the terrain is sparsely populated desert with no water or fuel points, in which security force patrols are rare. This is one of the reasons why Ellis liked to take along his own version of a desert still to make his own water in the event of his having to put down and being stranded.

Reasons for these anomalies are deep-seated. Puntland's air-wing operations are totally financed by and under the control of officials from the United Arab Emirates. While the Garowe-based Puntland Development Group (PDG) has the final say in most matters, there is little cooperation between the two principals, in part because of corruption on a massive scale.

It is no secret that pirates operating from Puntland make fair provision for many members of that government with any ransom money that is paid for ships released. A case in point is the $12 million handed over by Western owners for two ships and their crews that were released in 2013, of which a significant proportion went to Puntland ministers as well as heads of security services, including police chiefs. As a consequence, pirates operating from Puntland, until fairly recently, were free to operate in the adjacent Red Sea and Indian Ocean waters, almost with impunity.

Ellis also pointed at a significant amount of human trafficking into Puntland from the Yemen. Some of these victims were brought into the country in Arab dhows, but even when apprehended, the law is rarely allowed to take its course.

Five dhows with a large number of illegals were apprehended by the Alouette when Ellis still ran the air wing. They were escorted to Bosaso where the boats were impounded and their crews arrested. Yet inexplicably, both boats and crews were released weeks later, and allowed to leave the country without those involved being criminally charged. The word was that somebody in the Yemen had paid an 'incentive' to local officials for this to happen.

A notable success involving 'freelance aviators', when Arthur Walker was still in Bosaso, was the rescue of twenty-two sailors who had been held hostage by pirates on board the Panamanian-registered freighter *Iceberg* for three years. Several crew members of the crew had died in the interim, while others had been savaged and tortured by their Somali guards. The *Iceberg*'s chief engineer had had his ears cut off because he 'did not listen'. His incarcerators then crushed his leg with a steel bar so that he could not escape.

Aware of the fate of these men, the Puntland authorities tried to negotiate with the pirates, and indeed, they attempted to do so several times. However, their entreaties to release the prisoners were always rejected.

Finally, in December 2012, a small group of mercenaries in the employ of the Puntland Maritime Police Force (PMPF) attempted to rescue the prisoners. About twenty ground troops, including a Puntland detachment led by former Executive Outcomes veteran Rudolf van Heerden, with Puntland Rear Admiral Abdurizak Diri Farah in overall control, launched an attack. The effort was backed by Walker at the controls of the Alouette gunship flying top cover.

Al-Shabaab suspects guarded at a police station by SNA troops. (Photo Stuart Price)

Having brought some heavier weapons to bear, including a Russian 82mm smoothbore B-10 recoilless rifle and RPG-7s, the assault ended twelve days later when the pirates, using mobile phones, called their leaders to negotiate a truce through diplomatic channels in the Yemen.

Garowe agreed to exchange the hostages for the freedom of the pirates, the first time an independent military group had rescued a group of hostages from captivity while technically still at sea. The *Iceberg*, by then, had lost engine power and been driven ashore where it lay stranded. This development eventually resulted in an even deadlier threat being introduced into the security scenario.

With al-Qaeda-linked al-Shabaab forces having been driven out of some of their safe havens in southern Somalia, as a consequence of military ground and air action by African Union forces, Puntland experienced a surge of Islamist terrorism. Own sources indicate that there are now an estimated 300 al-Shabaab guerrilla fighters in Puntland alone, their ranks including several Egyptian jihadis.

Washington is aware of these developments following the withdrawal from Puntland of Bancroft Global Development, a military training group funded by the United Nations and the US State Department and headquartered in Washington DC and regionally in Mogadishu, that had provided training in a range of military services. This included a number of disciplines, from bomb disposal and sniper training, to supplying of military materiel and uniforms, which cumulatively forced the terror group to move into the area adjoining the Red Sea. In the interim, another American firm has been tasked to run security operations in Puntland. Several anti-pirate missions took place under its auspices.

Back in Puntland, the security assets of the PMPF are modest and hardly capable of dealing with the increased threat level. Prior to Bancroft pulling back to Mogadishu, a pair of upgraded Mil Mi-17s was ordered, but these were put on hold and only later delivered.

The force also lacks the support of the original 120 expatriate combatants fielded by Bancroft. Involved then was former US Navy Seal Erik Prince, founder and owner of Blackwater International who, for the Puntland operation, had partnered up with Lafras Luitingh, a former South African special forces operative who had originally been involved with Executive Outcomes. About twenty private military contractors remain, all part of the PMPF air-wing infrastructure.

Still at the unit's Bosaso air base, is an Antonov An-26 with a rotating Russian crew. This aircraft is routinely tasked to bring in supplies, troop rotation, and the delivery of fuel and equipment to PMPF elements on distant operations.

This includes dropping 44-gallon drums of fuel at sea for the three Zodiac RHIB (rigid-hulled inflatable boat) high-performance craft fitted with 400hp Volvo twin-screw inboards and DShK 12.7mm heavy machine guns mounted on their prows. All of them are used for anti-piracy operations by the PFMF. According to Ellis, Jet-A1 fuel is also dropped by parachute for the helicopter when needed.

Additionally, the PMPF has at its headquarters base at Bosaso three modified Ayres Thrush crop-spraying aircraft, armed with four-barrelled mini-guns capable of firing 4,000 rounds a minute and American-supplied underwing air-to-ground rockets. Adapted for close-air support roles and labelled V-1-A Vigilantes', the aircraft were originally developed for the US Department of State for anti-narcotics crop-spraying roles, NEDS (Narcotics Eradication Delivery System), in Central and South America and Southeast Asia. The machines are a useful adjunct to the limited airborne capability of the PMPF.

Another aviation element routinely spotted at the air base was a pair of military Russian-built Mil Mi-17s with upgraded 2,500hp engines. No photos were allowed to be taken anywhere near the base or of any of the American crew members. What was known was that one of the pilots was a woman, but the pilots had no contact with anybody linked to the PMPF. Instead, those flying the Mi-17s liaised solely with senior military officers within the Puntland government.

Interesting, the pair of Mi-17s had been completely modified to include Western avionics, which, by some accounts, is a first for the Russian helicopter. Its original clamshell rear doors were removed and a ramp installed, very much in line with what was originally sported by the French-built SA 321 Aérospatiale Super Frelon helicopter, in all probability to allow for the mounting of automatic weapons for firing out of the rear. The Mi-17s regularly used the same shooting range for training as the PMPF helicopter, which lies a short distance from Bosaso.

That was the situation until Ellis returned to South Africa in 2013. Yet while he was still operating out of Bosaso, a major al-Shabaab cell was uncovered near the town. The base has come under attack at least once in recent months.

It was not the first time this had happened. While Arthur Walker was still around, local residents reported the presence an Arab dhow, purportedly out of

British ship RFA *Fort Victoria* passes Mogadishu during Operation Capri, the counter-piracy effort off the Somalian coast. (Photo Ministry of Defence)

the Yemen. It had entered one of the lagoons along this stretch of the northern coast where it unloaded a cargo. When some local residents began to approach the boat, its contraband was hurriedly buried and the crew fled. In a search the following day, that involved the unit's helicopter and PMPF ground forces, a cache of arms was uncovered, but it soon became clear that only part of the weapons' shipment had been unloaded.

Recovered by the security forces were 220 RPG-7 grenades (but no launchers), 40kg of TNT (most likely for use in IEDs), 200 electric detonators incorporating the latest technology, four rolls of cordtex, and 20kg of ammonium nitrate in sacks, a fertilizer commonly used in the manufacture of explosives.

Also uncovered was a quantity of Russian B-9 (slightly smaller than the B-10 recoilless gun) ammunition, as well as boxes of AK-47 and PKM 7.62mm ammunition and hand grenades.

Another dimension to the Somali imbroglio in the north is the vast deposits of oil that have been discovered in a string of desert regions to the south of Bosaso. Although Puntland's President Abdiweli Mohamed Ali Gas visited Mogadishu in 2014 where he was well received by the president of the central government, the oil issue topped the agenda.

Differences over piracy featured prominently. For more than a decade, this issue has achieved a high-level international profile, resulting in several nations, including the US, India, Russia, France, Britain and other NATO countries and a dozen more, deploying warships around Somalia to protect shipping. China is now also involved in naval patrols.

Still more worrying is the fact that piracy is widely viewed by most people in Somalia as a socially acceptable and lucrative lifestyle, which has attracted to its ranks former fishermen, ex-militiamen, and technical experts needed to keep pirate boats and their mother ships at sea.

There are also many people there who are quite outspoken in their defence of attacks on foreign ships. They maintain, often with vehemence, that it is a justified response to illegal fishing and the illegal dumping of toxic waste along Somalia's long and poorly policed coastline.

What is ironic about these anomalies is that having established the Puntland Maritime Police Force as a reasonably effective body dedicated to countering piracy, those airmen, ground forces and support elements at Bosaso who are involved in these activities are actually working against the government that pays them.

Russian-built Mil Mi-17 helicopters. (Photo NATO)

Suspected pirates apprehended by a VBSS crew from the USS *Vella Gulf*. (Photo Jason R. Zalasky)

9. AL-SHABAAB

In an article, in Arabic, titled 'Al-Qaeda is Moving to Africa', Abu Azzam al-Ansari provides us with an analysis of all the possible advantages of Africa as a battlefield and a greenhouse for a global jihad.[1]

The report was innocuous enough because it was a minor article on page two of London's *Daily Telegraph*[2] a few days after Christmas, 2011.

Headed 'Met officers question terrorist suspect in Kenya', it referred to a team of officers from Scotland Yard sent to Kenya to talk to a British subject who had been arrested on charges of terrorism. The man had been arrested in Mombasa, on the Kenyan coast, on allegations that he was an explosives expert for the Somali jihadi group al-Shabaab.

There were seven others taken into custody with him, all accused of plotting to attack Westerners and their interests during the holiday season. Other reports spoke of cell members having been arrested after they crossed over from Somalia weeks before. Kenyan police were said to have raided a house used by the group, where they seized material and chemicals for making explosives.

A British Foreign Office spokesman said that its counter-terrorism officials had offered assistance to the Kenyans, adding that Britain's MI5 and Secret Intelligence Service, MI6 'had become aware of a number of young men arriving in the East African country from the United Kingdom to cross the border into Somalia'. Many of these youths were of Somali extraction and, once in Mogadishu, they joined up with al-Shabaab for military training, after which they would return to Britain. There was no comment as to why they would be going back to their British origins, or what ultimate purpose these moves would have.

There is now little doubt that al-Qaeda is on the move. Thwarted, in its bid to take over governments, such as Afghanistan and Pakistan, which have been mentioned in this context in the past, Osama bin Laden and his lieutenants originally moved sections of their strategic and logistical forces into Africa in the 1990s. Moreover, Western intelligence sources now concede that a revolutionary movement has developed in Somalia, where it is nurturing a powerful grip on what is left of the country's government.

SNA soldiers race along in an ubiquitous 'technical' in Mogadishu. (Photo AMISOM Public Information)

Al-Qaeda operatives are active in a number of other countries in the region. These include Eritrea, Chad, Kenya, Tanzania, Sudan, the Congo, and several West African countries.

To understand how all this has come about on the expansive fringes of the Indian Ocean, one has need to comprehend what is going on today in Somalia, an ungoverned and ungovernable swathe of largely arid real estate on the north-eastern Horn of Africa. It is also a region that dominates one of the busiest sea lanes of the world. Strategists on both sides of the Atlantic have warned for some years that this narrow waterway handles almost half the world's crude oil supplies from the Gulf, and that the region is becoming increasingly vulnerable.

An ongoing level of piracy that emanated in the past from Somalia underscores this concern, which is why almost two dozen countries, including Russia and China, have deployed significant naval units into the region. The task is enormous as, until recently, Somali pirates operated across an area several times the size of Europe.

In a report[3] titled 'The Talibanization of Somalia' by Abdi Abdi, an Ethiopian specialist in African and Islamic affairs, he alleged that al-Qaeda's activities in Somalia began as early as 1992. The organization's role during the course of the 1992–94 United Nations' missions was limited to a handful of trainers and, he added, Ali Mohamed and other al-Qaeda members purportedly trained forces loyal to warlord Mohammed Farah Aideed.

Osama bin Laden himself claimed, in an interview with ABC's John Miller, to have sent al-Qaeda operatives to Somalia. One of the al-Qaeda fighters present during the interview claimed to have personally slit the throats of three American soldiers in Somalia.[4]

Indeed, Mark Bowden declared that the terror organization trained some of Aidid's men, but that they were not personally part of the skirmish with American forces in the 1993 Battle of Mogadishu.

In 2002, another successful terrorist attack was launched in Kenya after the US Embassy bombing. This time it was a car bomb attack on a Mombasa resort hotel popular among Israeli tourists, which claimed the lives of fifteen people. It occurred only twenty minutes after a failed attack on a passenger jet when a terrorist fired a SAM-7 man-portable air-defence system against an Israeli airliner carrying 261 passengers, at the time in the process of taking off from Mombasa Airport. The missile seemingly failed to track its target. It failed to detonate, landing instead in an empty field.

Lately, a report headed 'Al-Qaeda Involvement in Africa', al-Shabaab was linked to the Somali militant Islamic Courts Union (ICU) front.[5] It states that several terrorist attacks were orchestrated from Ras Kamboni, in the extreme southern tip of Somalia, adjacent to Kenya, and included the 1998 US Embassy bombings and the 2002 Mombasa hotel bombing.

Jendayi Frazer, the then Assistant Secretary of State for African Affairs, announced that Washington was seeking the assistance of the ICU in the apprehension of the suspects who had carried out the attacks. She listed the following persons suspected of being in Somalia, shown by name and nationality: Fazul Abdullah Mohamed (Comoros), Saleh Ali Saleh Nabhan (Kenya) and Abu Taha al-Sudan (Sudan).

When the ICU did not cooperate, the United States first financed the rival warlord factions, followed with limited air strikes as the ICU rule in Mogadishu collapsed in the face of an Ethiopian army assault.

Kenyan AMISOM troops in front of the damaged Kismayo airport building, daubed with the black al-Shabaab flag. (Photo Stuart Price)

The Pentagon disclosed in a public briefing that a high level al-Qaeda member from the ICU was captured in Somalia and transferred to the US military prison at Guantanamo Bay.[6]

Considering the political impasse in the region, vis-à-vis Islamic insurgency, East Africa deserves much more attention by the major powers. This coastal area stretches from Somalia southward all the way to Mozambique and includes a traditional, mainly Omani Islamic community that goes back centuries, founded on the original trade in spices and slaves between Africa and the Middle East. The entire region is now being subverted.

There are several other threats, including those involving weapons of mass destruction. It consequently makes good sense to recap at this point on the long-term nuclear potential of several African and contiguous Islamic states, underscored by David Albright's book *Peddling Peril: How the Secret Nuclear Trade Arms America's Enemies*, published by New York's The Free Press in 2010.

President of Washington's Institute for Science and International Security, David Albright, declared that al-Qaeda and additional hostile groups in failed states might be able to import the equipment and materials to cobble together a crude atomic weapon.

That followed former CIA director George Tenet's warning that 'in the current marketplace, if you have a hundred million dollars, you have your own nuclear power.'

From an early age, Osama bin Laden was worth an estimated half a billion dollars, accrued from family-oriented construction projects, without which he would never have been able to fund many of the projects on which al-Qaeda had embarked. More recently, Saudi grassroots revolutionary-level Wahhabist

Member of a combat engineering team checking for IEDs outside a mosque, Mogadishu. (Photo Stuart Price)

Al-Shabaab photos showing the January 2016 capture and destruction of a Kenyan Army base in southern Somalia, in which at least 65 Kenyan troops were killed and several captured. Al-Shabaab claimed over 100 Kenyans were killed.

elements have been providing the wherewithal for some of these actions. The cost, reckoned by some intelligence specialists in London and Washington, runs into hundreds of millions of dollars a year.

There have been a number of successes, including the uncovering of a major al-Qaeda network along the Kenyan coast.

Kenya security elements, including its police force, working in conjunction with Western security groups, have seized large numbers of weapons, training manuals and terrorist safe houses. These raids were followed by the arrest of dozens of suspects wanted for several al-Qaeda attacks in East Africa, including some on the FBI's most-wanted list.

Several news reports from Reuters, Agence France Presse, the Associated Press and others have appeared in recent years, all underscoring the presence of powerful al-Qaeda political and military elements in Somalia. The quantity and quality of weapons being smuggled into Somalia has also been upgraded, with the intention of carrying out more terrorist attacks in Kenya and its neighbours. At the time, much of this hardware was brought across from the Yemen by Arab sailing ships (dhows). The civil war in that Arab country has impeded but not halted this movement.

Somalis have moved into many parts of east and southern Africa in considerable numbers over past decades, some legitimately into their countries of choice, though many more of them illegal immigrants who survive by paying bribes to government officials who are so poorly paid that these gratuities are factored into their household budgets as a matter of course.

More worrying, tens of thousands of Somalis have managed to acquire Kenyan passports, and are today registered members of the Kenyan community.

The majority of Somalis resident in Kenya, as with their fellow countrymen in Europe and North America, tend to retain their Somali identities, often preferring to speak their own language in preference to those of their adopted countries, or rather, the countries that have embraced them. They also remain staunchly Muslim, which is why youthful Somalis are sometimes persuaded to return to their homeland to join the largely anti-Western revolution to undergo military training.

The *Washington Times* in June 2010 carried a major report about al-Qaeda recruits in Africa, stating that parts of East Africa had become a major recruiting ground for Islamist militants.[7] In the dispatch, Ted Dagne, an African-affairs specialist, declared that al-Qaeda and its allies 'are much stronger today than they were a few years ago'. Also mentioned in the report by Ashish

Kumar, United States intelligence officials 'have expressed concerns about the terrorist threat posed by the Horn of Africa'.

The Somali conundrum in Kenya is regarded by some observers that the author spoke to in Nairobi as a significant problem for the future, in part, because so many of these Hamitic people are there quite honourably while pursuing perfectly legitimate business. They are part of the local social scene. Their children go to Kenyan schools and universities, while some even have government jobs, including in the military or security.

Many of these people live in Eastleigh, one of Nairobi's largest suburbs, long regarded by both London and Washington as being at the heart of subversive al-Qaeda activity in East Africa.[8]

London's Chatham House has dealt with an aspect of the economic side of things in a report written by Farah Abdulsamed in March 2011, headed, 'Somali Investment in Kenya'. Centred on the Nairobi suburb of Eastleigh, the document provides an interesting backdrop.[9]

Chatham House stated that many Kenyans believed there was a strong relationship between Somali investors and the pirates and warlords of Somalia. While the Kenyan media have produced some wildly exaggerated reports, there are certainly some properties owned by pirates and warlords in Nairobi and Mombasa. Kenya's weak anti-money-laundering legislation and enforcement make Nairobi an attractive destination for this activity.

What is significant is that Eastleigh, once a predominantly Asian residential estate, has drawn a lot of attention from British and American intelligence operatives because it is through there that many radical Somalis – particularly those with ties to the al-Qaeda-linked al-Shabaab terror organization – gravitate abroad.

While difficult to establish accurately, it was estimated by some authoritative sources such as the United Nations High Commission for Refugees (UNHCR) that by 2010 Eastleigh's Somali population had topped the quarter million mark, in large part because the civil war back home that broke out in 1991 forced many Somalis to seek asylum in Somali-inhabited enclaves in Kenya, Eastleigh in particular.

This was not an altogether negative development since the Somali people are traditionally an entrepreneurial community. They established themselves in the Nairobi business sector, investing more than $1.5 billion in Eastleigh alone.

Former US Secretary of State John Kerry and survivor Rukiya Ali lay a wreath at the August 7 Memorial Park, Nairobi, in memory of the 213 killed in the terror attack on the US Embassy on 7 August 1998. (Photo US State Department)

Following government pressure that started in late 2012, following various Somali terror links throughout East Africa, a mass exodus of Somali residents was reported after a prolonged period of harassment by the Kenyan police and public. The collective departures most affected Eastleigh's real estate sector, as landlords struggled to find Kenyans able to afford the high rentals of the apartments and shops vacated by the Somalis.

As the Chatham House report declared, funds from the wider Somali diaspora have been crucial to the expansion of Eastleigh. Commercial-mall companies such as Amal, Baraka Bazaar, Garissa Lodge and Sunshine Plaza are in this category, with annual turnover of no more than $7 million. Many entrepreneurs who began in the informal economy have expanded their businesses, turning them into contemporary shopping malls, operating inside the formal economy.

In reality, warns the report out of London, the value of Somali trade and investment in Kenya is much larger than the proceeds of piracy. Anecdotal evidence points to investments of over $1.5 billion in Eastleigh in 2004. Ransoms in 2009 were estimated at around $100 million. Property prices in these Kenyan business areas rose because of growing demand, but residential property prices appeared to be lower in areas dominated by Somalis. Somali businessmen in Kenya dismissed these complaints and attribute them to people who feel threatened by the success of Somali businesses.

In a section headed 'Investments turn bad – the Dalsan case', Chatham House pointed to Somali networks of family trusts as having been very effective at producing capital and returns. It went on:

> Sometimes the unregulated nature of much of this activity can provide cover for fraud and, some suspect, the funding of armed groups.
>
> The Dalsan hawala service was, at its height, transferring up to $100 million a year; yet in 2006 the company folded and investors and customers lost tens of millions of dollars. Like other Somali business people the founders of Dalsan sold shares to Somalis across the globe. Much of the fundraising was carried out through mosques, and Dalsan expanded across Somalia, Africa, Europe and North America.

There are other, more serious factors. A US State Department report titled 'Arms and Conflict in Africa', declared that at the present time there are a dozen major conflicts taking place on this vast continent, with a number of smaller wars smouldering, more than on anywhere else on the globe. Some of these brushfire wars don't even make the news.[10]

Taken together, these hostilities have produced more than eight million refugees in the past decade. The number of dead in the débâcle that is the present-day Democratic Republic of the Congo is estimated to be between four and five million dead.

'The proliferation of light weapons financed by cash, diamonds and other commodities did not cause Africa's wars,' the report warned. Instead, 'it has prolonged them and made them more lethal.'

It went on to suggest that any society that has thugs on street corners selling automatic weapons at $6 a throw has serious problems.

Conventional weapons such as AK-47 assault rifles are selling for that in several African states, Washington disclosed, and Somalia is being used as a conduit for much of it. Hardware available to foment revolution includes rocket-propelled grenades, mortars and landmines. In this regard, Kenya, Ethiopia, Eritrea, the Sudan, the Central African Republic, Tanzania, the Congo and several countries farther afield, are affected, with al-Qaeda-linked Somali dissidents operating in many of them.

The easy availability of cheap, light weapons has made more conflicts in Africa inevitable, the document revealed, adding that the troubled continent had become 'the world's small-arms dumping ground in the aftermath of the Cold War'. This is a scenario that is almost tailor-made for those of the more fundamentalist Islamic revolutionary ilk.

One of the consequences of what took place in the Congo was Ted Koppel's emotional mea culpa television series on that sad land. The most salient question he raised was how, in these modern times, could so many people have been so brutally murdered in the Congo without anybody taking notice, or, more to point, protesting such dreadful human-rights excesses.

The truth is that al-Qaeda flourishes when there is dislocation and mayhem. That is adequately underscored by the ongoing war in Afghanistan, coupled with a level of insecurity and subversion in Pakistan that has the West seriously concerned. It is worth recalling that prior to the invasion of Afghanistan by coalition forces, Osama bin Laden was visited by several Pakistani nuclear scientists after he had told A.Q. Khan, Pakistan's criminal nuclear proliferator, that he wished to acquire the bomb. As one wag phrased it, 'the situation was roughly akin to an Upper Volta with nukes.'

Which brings us back to security elements linked to the Mogadishu government – such as it is – and intended to counter the activities of the al-Shabaab terror group in Somalia itself.

The Joshua Meservey and Kelsey Lilley report 'Is the Coalition Fighting al-Shabaab Falling Apart?' quoted in the previous chapter, made a number of salient comments about the structure of the African Union force and its finances.[11] These are some of the more important issues covered:

> The domestic woes of the most prominent troop-contributing countries vary, but all have the potential to disrupt the AMISOM mission. Burundi, a small country that punches above its weight with its 5,400 soldiers deployed throughout Somalia, remains trapped in a long-simmering domestic political crisis. In response to the Burundian government's violent handling of pro-democracy demonstrators, the European Union cut $484 million in aid to Burundi in 2016 and threatened to pull another $65 million in annual commitments to the country's AMISOM contingent. If these threats compel a Burundian withdrawal, or if the Burundian government decides its troops would be more useful at home, AMISOM would suffer a serious blow.

The report also drew attention to shortcomings suffered by the Ugandan AMISOM contingent of 6,000 troops which President Yoweri Museveni threatened to withdraw. This would be a serious loss because the Ugandans, by and large a strong, disciplined military group, have played an exemplary security role in countering al-Shabaab advances in Somalia in recent years.

For all that, maintains the Joshua Meservey and Kelsey Lilley report, Museveni is likely uninclined to leave AMISOM at present 'because he wishes to maintain his position as a regional power broker. Yet without progress in the Somali security sector, he may come to believe Uganda's participation is untenable'. It goes on:

> Kenya, which contributes about 3,500 troops to AMISOM, may have a larger stake in the Somali political order than most other countries in this coalition. Kenya has suffered repeated al-Shabaab terrorist attacks inside its borders, and its long-standing plan to repatriate hundreds of thousands of Somali refugees relies on a semblance of stability in southern Somalia. The Kenyan military is also accused of making millions of dollars by smuggling sugar and charcoal through Somalia's port of Kismayo, which it controls and is likely keen to hold on to.

More recently, the Nairobi government has given notice that it intends to repatriate a large proportion of the almost two million Somali refugees in Kenya back to their home country, starting with the community held in Dadaab, a semi-arid town in Garissa County, Kenya, the site of a UNHCR base hosting more than a quarter of million refugees in five camps as of January 2017. That makes it the largest such complex in the world.

Amnesty International, which is among several groups that challenged the government's actions, said the closure of Dadaab would leave more than 260,000 Somali refugees with nowhere to go. That was followed by Kenya's High Court ruling that the government could not unilaterally shut down the world's largest refugee camp because it was contrary to fundamental human rights to which Kenya has unequivocally subscribed since independence in 1963.

At the time of going to press, the situation remains in a state of impasse.

It is worth mentioning that the inability of some Western countries, especially the United States, to understand the fundamental mindset of the average Somali – particularly in those rebel elements operating with an organization like al-Shabaab – is also at issue here.

SNA soldier on security and anti IED operations in Torfiq market, northern Mogadishu. (Photo Stuart Price)

Clearly, this state of affairs is going to remain fluid for the foreseeable future.

John Amble, a PhD candidate at the Institute of Middle Eastern Studies at King's College London and former US Army intelligence officer and veteran of Iraq and Afghanistan, who writes on international terrorism, and related intelligence, replied to an article that appeared in the *Washington Post* under the heading 'The Challenge of al-Shabaab in Somalia'.[12]

Critical of an op-ed piece written by Michael Shank and titled 'Our Moral Obligations in Somalia', Amble makes it pretty clear that Shank knows very little about what is really going on in Africa's Horn, and specifically Somalia.

Shank argues that the United States 'fails to understand the challenge posed by Islamist militant group al-Shabaab, and consequently squanders opportunities to contribute to the country's stabilization.' He agrees that much of what Shank writes is generally accurate and is clearly knowledgeable about the country but he takes him to task for characterizing the bulk of al-Shabaab recruits as unemployed, impoverished youth.

This is absolutely correct, agrees Amble, adding:

But his implication that this contradicts an assessment of the threat the group poses to regional security and stability is naïve. Lack of opportunity might well be among the most important drivers of al-Shabaab recruitment, but this doesn't alter the core identity or mission of a group.

Much of its leadership is committed to a global Jihadist ideology, and all of its leadership is committed to introducing Islamist governance into a society for which it is culturally a poor fit. This argument is the functional equivalent to discounting any expansionist threat posed by the Soviet Union because most Red Army soldiers were not true believers in worldwide socialist revolution.

Second, Shank argues that the US has an immediate opportunity to promote stability in Somalia. 'But it requires a serious rethink on how we wage war,' he writes. 'In Somalia, a war on poverty and unemployment would go a lot farther in meeting our objectives than our current stategy.'

Yes, says Amble, policies geared toward combating poverty and unemployment hold very real, significant potential, but they are not mutually exclusive with a kinetic counterterrorism strategy, adding that by implying otherwise suggests an unbalanced appreciation of the efficacy of the various tools of power and influence at a government's disposal. He concludes, 'Finally, Shank maintains that an immediate goal of US policy should be to "ensure that Somalia's president and prime minister's spots, ministerial posts, and members of parliament are better balanced, more inclusive, and more representative, as they have, for decades, been dominated by a few clans only".'

Amble:

The notion that the international community can impose a political system consistent with its views of democracy and fair representation fails to acknowledge that it was precisely this approach that has underpinned failed attempts to stabilize Somalia for two decades. An endless succession of internationally sponsored peace conferences and reconciliation agreements reached in Djibouti, Nairobi, Addis Ababa, and elsewhere have yielded incremental progress at best, and produced the much-maligned 4.5 formula of clan power division.

Kenyan troops and the Somali Ras Kamboni Brigade march on Kismayo. (Photo Stuart Price)

Yet Shank seems to believe that a similar effort by the United States and other world powers is now the most appropriate prescription for Somalia's lingering challenges.

> To be sure, US policy toward Somalia has not achieved the objectives of promoting stability and security toward which it is geared. But this Op-Ed's conclusions are based on an inaccurate appreciation of both local dynamics and two decades of international policy toward the country. As such, it does little to inform a more effective strategic approach to combating al-Shabaab and stabilizing Somalia.'

In the view of this author, the issues debated remains one of most intractable problems of the modern age and one of the reasons why, on going to press, there were almost 50,000 more Somalis waiting to enter the United States and who knows how many more heading towards Europe.

NOTES

Chapter 1

1 Bamber Gascoigne: 'History of Somalia': www.historyworld.net/wrldhis/PlainTextHistories.asp?historyid=ad20

2 Elri Liebenberg: 'The Springboks in East Africa: The Role of 1 SA Survey Company (SAEC) in the East African Campaign of World War II, 1940-1941', *Scientia Militaria: South African Journal of Military Studies*, 2016.

3 www.enoughproject.org/blogs/somalia-colonialism-independence-dictatorship-1840-1976.

4 Molly Zapata's blog: 'Somalia – Colonialism to Independence to Dictatorship 1840–1976', posted 31 January, 2012.

Chapter 3

1. Venter, Al J., *The Chopper Boys: Helicopter Warfare in Africa*, Casemate Publishers (US), Greenhill Books (UK), Southern Books (South Africa), 1994.

Chapter 7

1. Bryce, Robert, 'Man Versus Mine', Foreign Affairs, *The Atlantic Monthly*, January/February, 2006.

2. UN Transitional Authority in Cambodia.

Chapter 8

1. *Jane's Defence Weekly*, London, posted online 13 March 2014. Hardcopy version in issue dated 19 March 2014.

2. There are several chapters that cover the late Arthur Walker's role in these guerrilla struggles in the author's book, *War Dog: Fighting Other People's Wars*, published by Casemate in the US and UK in 2006. Walker succumbed to cancer in 2016.

Chapter 9

1. Paz, Reuven, and Terdman, Moshe, *Africa: The Gold Mine of Al-Qaeda and Global Jihad, The Project for the Research of Islamist Movements* (PRISM) Vol. 4 (2006) No. 2 (June 2006). Abu Azzam al-Ansari: *al-Qaeda tattajih*

nahwa Ifrikya (Al Qaeda is Moving to Africa) *Sada al-Jihad*, No. 7 (June 2006) pp 27–30.

2. Heaton, Laura, in Nairobi, and Hardham, Duncan, 'Met Officers to Question Suspect in Kenya': *Daily Telegraph*, London, 28 December 2011.

3. Abdi, Abdi, 'The Talibanization of Somalia', Ethiopian News Agency, 12 July 2006.

4. 'Pentagon Captures High Level al-Qaeda Member in Somalia', BBC News (http://news.bbc.co.uk/2/hi/africa/67290.stm).

5. http://en-wikipedia.org/wike/Al-Qaeda_involvement_in_Africa.

6. 'US Seeks Islamic Courts Help to Catch Somali Extremists', *Somaliland Times*, 23 June 2006

7. Sen, Ashish Kumar, 'Al-Qaeda Recruits in Africa', *Washington Times*, 17 June 2010

8. Personal communications with individuals in London and Washington who do not wish to be identified.

9. Abdulsamed, Farah, Chatham House, 'Somali Investment in Kenya', Africa Program, March 2011 (AFP BP 2011/02).

10. US State Department: 'Arms and Conflict in Africa', Washington DC, 2005.

11. Meservey, Joshua, policy analyst, Africa and the Middle East at the Heritage Foundation and Lilley, Kelsey, associate director of the Atlantic Council's Africa Centre in the United States, 'Is the Coalition Fighting al-Shabaab Falling Apart?'

12. Amble, John, Letters to the Editor, *Washington Post* 'The Challenge of al-Shabaab in Somalia', 19 August 2013.

ACKNOWLEDGEMENTS

My assignments to Somalia over the years – except the time I took my wife to Mogadishu – were always 'in and out' affairs. I would head in solo, largely to attract as little attention as possible, do what was needed and fly out again. It was comparatively easy before the civil war started but once the Soviets were ensconced throughout the country, things became more difficult. Being Westerners, we were constantly under surveillance.

During the course of my first few visits, my old Nairobi *rafiki* Mohammad Amin would smooth the way, usually with one of his stringers or fixers who lived there. But then, after hostilities had started and there were many indiscriminate murders, I tended to work things out for myself. That was a time when you could buy an AK-47 off the shelf in downtown Mogadishu for $100: a box of ammo came with it, no charge.

It was different after the Americans had moved in with Operation Just Hope under the UNOSOM mantle. In charge of media was a US Marine half-colonel Fred Peck, a great guy who expressed surprise that someone in the US State Department had given me his name. I explained that I was in the final stages of putting together *The Chopper Boys*, my book about helicopter warfare in Africa and that I was not interested in Somalia's 'starving millions', but rather, was eager to spend a bit of time with some of the American helicopter units then active in-country. He looked me over briefly, smiled and turned to an aide. 'Let's get this man to Baledogle soonest possible. They'll give him what he wants.' The strip had been a former Soviet air station and lies in the desert interior just a short chopper hop from Mogadishu.

Running the show, or part of it, was Major Pauline Knapp who spent much of her time flying UH-60 Blackhawk choppers. She commanded the US Army Aero Medical Evacuation Company. An extremely competent aviator, Pauline pulled out all stops and I went on quite a few missions with some of the fly boys and girls who were more actively involved in Somali 'hostilities'.

Once at Baledogle, Colonel Mike Dallas, commander of the 2nd Brigade, 10th Mountain Division at the air base assisted where he could, though he warned when I arrived that the base was 'dry' and also that smoking was only grudgingly tolerated.

That was when my new-found buddy, Chief Warrant Officer Dave Coates – who flew AH-1 Cobras against dissident groups of Somalis in the interior – kept me supplied with his secret supply of grog, hidden in a very cleverly concealed chamber behind his unit's portable pantry.

Somebody else who subsequently helped was Captain Robert Doss, a US Marine mission planner and CH-46E Sea Knight helicopter pilot. He gave me all he could on Operation Eastern Exit which, before UNOSOM, was involved in an enormously complicated night-time evacuation of US embassy staff from the American compound on the outskirts of Mogadishu, by then under heavy rebel fire. In the end the Americans evacuated scores of diplomatic personnel from other embassies in the Somali capital, flown out to US carriers waiting offshore. It went off like a charm without a single casualty, though there was an awful lot of enemy firepower deployed against the rescuers.

The author at Baledogle during the US-led Operation Just Hope.

ABOUT THE AUTHOR

Al J. Venter is a specialist military writer who has had fifty books published. He started his career with Geneva's Interavia Group, then owners of *International Defence Review*, to cover military developments in the Middle East and Africa. Venter has been writing on these and related issues such as guerrilla warfare, insurgency, the Middle East and conflict in general for half a century. He was involved with Jane's Information Group for more than thirty years. He was a stringer for the BBC, NBC News (New York), as well as London's *Daily Express* and *Sunday Express*. He branched into television work in the early 1980s, producing more than 100 documentaries, many of which were internationally flighted. His one-hour film, *Africa's Killing Fields*, on the Ugandan civil war, was shown nationwide in the United States on the PBS network. Other films include an hour-long programme on the fifth anniversary of the Soviet invasion of Afghanistan, as well as *AIDS: The African Connection*, which was nominated for China's Pink Magnolia Award. His last major book was *Portugal's Guerrilla Wars in Africa*, nominated in 2013 for New York's Arthur Goodzeit military history book award. It has gone into three editions, including translation into Portuguese.

5 - Mogadiscio - Museo della Garesa

Mogadiscio - Panoramica dal mare